THE CONFLICT WITH ISIS:
Operation INHERENT RESOLVE

JUNE 2014–JANUARY 2020

BY

MASON W. WATSON

Center of Military History
United States Army
Washington, D.C. 2021

THE U.S. ARMY CAMPAIGNS IN IRAQ

The Surge, 2007–2008

The Conflict with ISIS: Operation INHERENT RESOLVE, *June 2014–January 2020*

Cover: *An Iraqi Counter Terrorism Service convoy moves toward Mosul, Iraq, 23 February 2017.* (U.S. Army)

CMH Pub 78–2

INTRODUCTION

Between 2003 and 2011, the terrorist group known as al-Qaeda in Iraq (AQI) was among the most dangerous and brutal elements in the Iraqi insurgency that arose following the collapse of Saddam Hussein's regime. Led by the Jordanian jihadist Abu Musab al-Zarqawi, AQI sought to provoke a sectarian conflict that would destroy the newly democratic Iraqi government and allow for the formation of a self-proclaimed "Islamic state." Iraqi government forces, supported by a U.S.-led coalition, managed to suppress the civil unrest and brought AQI to the brink of total defeat by 2010. However, the U.S. withdrawal from Iraq the following year, combined with the outbreak of a civil war in neighboring Syria, enabled the terrorist group to stage a comeback. In the summer of 2014, AQI—rebranded as the Islamic State of Iraq and Syria (ISIS)—launched an offensive that brought around one-third of Iraq under its control. At the same time, it carved out a similarly large territory in Syria.

The United States dubbed its military response to these events Operation INHERENT RESOLVE. Rather than deploying large formations to fight ISIS directly, as the United States had done in Afghanistan and during the earlier stages of the conflict in Iraq, the Barack H. Obama and Donald J. Trump administrations eschewed a major ground combat mission against the Islamic State. Instead, they provided strong support to local proxies, who did most of the fighting. This approach proved successful, limiting American casualties and the financial cost of the conflict. The efforts of U.S. Army trainers, military advisers, and small combat elements, reinforced by coalition counterparts and backed by American airpower, enabled Iraqi and Syrian forces to liberate all of the territory held by ISIS by March 2019.

3

With this series of commemorative pamphlets, the U.S. Army Center of Military History aims to provide soldiers and civilians with an overview of operations in the wars after 11 September 2001 and to remember the hundreds of thousands of U.S. Army personnel who served on behalf of their nation. These publications are dedicated to them.

JON T. HOFFMAN
Chief Historian

Operation INHERENT RESOLVE

JUNE 2014–JANUARY 2020

Early in the morning of 18 December 2011, a convoy of 110 U.S. military vehicles and 500 soldiers from the 3d Brigade Combat Team, 1st Cavalry Division, crossed over the Iraqi border and entered Kuwait.[1] The departure of these troops signaled the end of almost nine years of U.S. military operations in Iraq. President Barack H. Obama heralded the moment as the conclusion of "one of the most extraordinary chapters in the history of the American military." The future of Iraq, he said, "will be in the hands of its people. America's war in Iraq will be over."[2] Within three years, however, the fragile Iraqi state was fighting for its life. Taking advantage of the spiraling civil war in Syria and sectarian strife in Iraq, a militant group known as the Islamic State of Iraq and Syria (ISIS) mustered an irregular but well-organized military force and launched an offensive against the Iraqi government in January 2014.* By the end of June, the group controlled a territory roughly the size of Kentucky, spanning Iraq and Syria. Around eleven million people found themselves under the rule

---

* The Islamic State has gone by several different names during its existence. Originally founded in 1999 as the Group of Monotheism and Jihad, the organization changed its name to "al-Qaeda in Iraq" (AQI) in 2004 when it became affiliated with al-Qaeda Central. In 2006, the group renamed itself the Islamic State of Iraq. In 2013, following its expansion into Syria, it became the Islamic State of Iraq and al-Sham. As al-Sham is sometimes translated as "Levant," an alternative acronym for the group during this period is ISIL. Also sometimes used is the Arabic abbreviation "Daesh," equivalent to ISIL or ISIS. In 2014, the group dropped all regional designations, becoming simply the Islamic State. For clarity, this pamphlet follows U.S. military usage, referring to the group as "al-Qaeda in Iraq" or "AQI" between 1999 and 2013, and after as "ISIS" or "the Islamic State."

Map 1

of this self-declared "Islamic State."[3] From their new base in the Iraqi city of Mosul, ISIS forces pushed south toward Baghdad, threatening not only the national integrity of Iraq but also the security and stability of the entire Middle East.

In mid-June 2014, President Obama ordered American troops to return to Iraq as the spearhead of what would become Operation INHERENT RESOLVE (OIR)—the military campaign to degrade and destroy the Islamic State. They operated as part of a new command, Combined Joint Task Force–Operation INHERENT RESOLVE (CJTF-OIR). By early 2019, Iraqi and Syrian forces— supported by U.S. airpower, armed with U.S. equipment, and trained and assisted by U.S. military advisers—had defeated ISIS forces on the battlefield and ended the group's pretentions to statehood. American forces under CJTF-OIR then transitioned to supporting local partners in Iraq and Syria as they worked to stabilize liberated areas and combat the remnants of the ISIS insurgency.

STRATEGIC SETTING

Iraq is geographically, religiously, and ethnically diverse. The Tigris and Euphrates Rivers, flowing southeast from Turkey and merging about 200 kilometers from the Persian Gulf, define the country's terrain. Much of Iraq's population and nearly all of its major cities lie along the two rivers. Baghdad, the capital, straddles the Tigris in the country's central region. Other major urban centers include Mosul in the north and Al Basrah near the Persian Gulf. The sparsely populated Syrian Desert dominates western Iraq, the Al-Jazeera uplands cover the expanse between the Tigris and the Euphrates in the northwest, and the Zagros Mountains and their foothills dominate the northeast. Iraq borders Iran to the east, Turkey to the north, Syria to the northwest, Jordan to the west, and Saudi Arabia and Kuwait to the south (*Map 1*).

The majority of Iraq's thirty-two million inhabitants adhere to one of the two major branches of Islam: around 30 percent are Sunni and around 60 percent are Shi'a. Linguistic, cultural, and ethnic differences distinguish Arab Iraqis of both sects—about 80 percent of the population—from the largely Sunni Kurds, who live mainly in the autonomous Kurdistan region in the country's northeast. Less than 1 percent of the population belongs to other minority groups—including Yazidis, Christians, Assyrians, and Turkomans—most of whom live in the northwest. Sunni Arabs constitute a majority of the population in the west, while Shi'as predominate in central and southern Iraq (*Map 2*).[4]

FROM INVASION TO WITHDRAWAL

Iraq has been in a state of almost continuous conflict since 1980. After a bloody eight-year war against Iran, Iraqi dictator Saddam Hussein invaded Kuwait in 1990, precipitating the first Persian Gulf War. An international coalition led by the United States swiftly defeated the Iraqi military and liberated Kuwait in 1991 but left Saddam in power. Throughout the following decade,

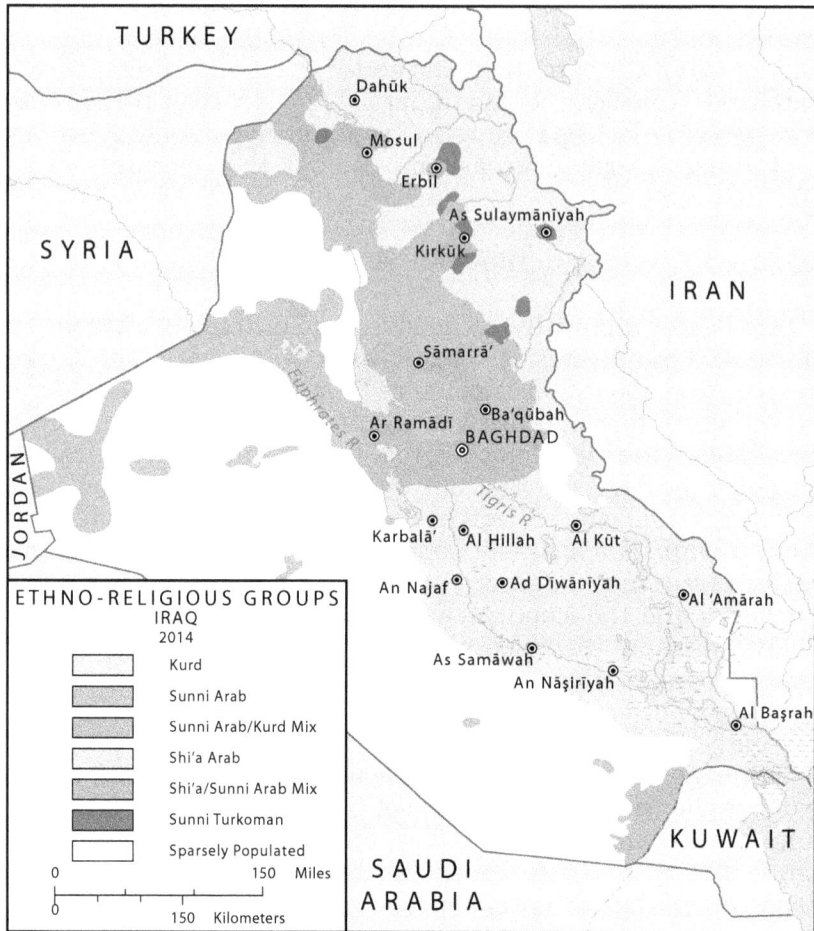

ETHNO-RELIGIOUS GROUPS
IRAQ
2014

- Kurd
- Sunni Arab
- Sunni Arab/Kurd Mix
- Shi'a Arab
- Shi'a/Sunni Arab Mix
- Sunni Turkoman
- Sparsely Populated

0   150   Miles

0   150   Kilometers

Map 2

U.S. and coalition forces maintained a forward presence in the region to deter Iraq from further acts of aggression.[5] In 2003, acting on intelligence that suggested that Iraq possessed—or was creating—weapons of mass destruction, the United States under President George W. Bush invaded Iraq and overthrew Saddam Hussein with the support of another international coalition. Designated Operation IRAQI FREEDOM, the campaign helped establish Iraq's first democratic government in more than fifty years and empowered the country's long-oppressed Shi'a majority. However, many Sunni Arabs felt that the U.S.-backed government had disenfranchised them, and their growing resentment fueled an insurgency against the American forces and the new Iraqi leadership. Shi'a and Sunni Iraqis also engaged in a sectarian civil war that included the religious "cleansing" of large areas before ending in a de facto Shi'a victory. Estimates of the number of Iraqis who died in the violence from 2003 through the U.S. withdrawal in 2011 range from 200,000 to more than a million.[6]

By August 2010, however, coalition and Iraqi forces appeared to have defeated the insurgency. The most dangerous insurgent group threat—Abu Musab al-Zarqawi's al-Qaeda in Iraq (AQI)—was in disarray. Al-Zarqawi himself was dead, killed by U.S. special operations forces in June 2006. His successor, Abu Ayyub al-Masri, died in a joint U.S. and Iraqi raid in April 2010. Membership in the organization dwindled to less than 1,000. Fighters who avoided death or detention at the hands of U.S. and Iraqi forces fled across the border into Syria. Some disillusioned insurgents even changed sides and joined forces with the Iraqi government to fight their former comrades. With insurgent forces demoralized and in disarray, violence declined to levels unseen since the invasion.[7]

Having helped to suppress the insurgent threat and lessen the likelihood of civil war in Iraq, the United States prepared to withdraw its forces. Operation IRAQI FREEDOM ended on 31 August 2010. Its successor, Operation NEW DAWN, involved the final transition of security responsibility from the United States military to the U.S.-trained Iraqi Security Forces (ISF). After the last U.S. combat troops departed in December 2011, the United States took steps to normalize its relations with Iraq for the first time since the invasion of Kuwait in 1990. The American presence in the country was limited to the U.S. embassy and its associated entities, including a small security cooperation cell.[8]

Without the continued support of U.S. military forces, however, it was not clear whether Iraq would remain stable. Violence began to increase in 2011, and the division between Sunni and Shi'a Iraqis remained acute. Unfortunately, the Shi'a-dominated government of Prime Minister Nouri Kamal al-Maliki showed little inclination to reach out to the Sunni population and make the kind of concessions that would promote reconciliation.[9] Compounding the country's internal tensions, the 929,000-strong Iraqi military still had significant weaknesses. Built from scratch by the United States at the cost of $25 billion, Iraq's armed forces depended on direct American assistance for essential functions, including logistics support; maintenance; and intelligence, surveillance, and reconnaissance.[10] Responsibility

9

for providing this support after 2011 devolved on the embassy's Office of Security Cooperation–Iraq (OSC-I), commanded by Lt. Gen. Robert L. Caslen. Although coalition planners originally conceived of OSC-I as a division-sized command, the office experienced severe personnel and funding reductions when the United States and Iraq failed to negotiate a new Status of Forces Agreement in October 2011. On the date of the official American withdrawal, OSC-I consisted of just 157 military personnel and 763 contractors. With limited resources, OSC-I confined itself to the activities typically performed by U.S. embassy security cooperation cells, including the management of foreign military sales and financing, senior leader engagements, and small-scale training exercises. The office also oversaw limited training of Iraqi units at outlying sites, mostly performed by contractors. These activities paled in comparison to the full-scale security force assistance program previously operated by the coalition military headquarters in Iraq.[11] The long-term consequences of this sharp—and unanticipated—reduction in assistance were as yet unknown.

THE RISE OF THE ISLAMIC STATE

On 7 March 2012, the commander of U.S. Central Command (CENTCOM), General James N. Mattis, testified before Congress that he had "never witnessed it so tumultuous" in the Middle

Arab Spring demonstration in Homs, Syria, April 2011
(*Bo yaser, Wikimedia Commons*)

Map 3

East.[12] The 2011 Arab Spring protest movement, which spurred the collapse of several long-established authoritarian regimes in Middle Eastern and North African countries such as Egypt and Tunisia, was a key cause of this regional instability. Iraq saw few Arab Spring protests, but demonstrations against the Ba'athist dictatorship of Syrian President Bashar al-Assad led to the outbreak of a civil war on Iraq's northwestern border.

About the size of Washington State, Syria is bounded by the Mediterranean Sea to the west, the countries of Lebanon, Israel, and Jordan in the south, Iraq in the east, and Turkey in the north. The Euphrates River, which cuts diagonally across Syria from northwest to southeast, separates the northeastern third of the country from the other two-thirds. Mountain ranges dominate northwestern and western Syria. Southeastern Syria along the Jordanian and Iraqi borders is mostly desert, and sparsely populated outside of the Euphrates River Valley (*Map 3*).

No major geographic features divide Iraq from Syria, and local tribes count citizens of both countries among their members.

As of 2011, Syria was home to approximately 21 million people. Around 80 percent of Syrians were ethnically Arab, and 60 percent adhered to Sunni Islam. A range of minority religious groups accounted for the remaining 40 percent of the country's population. Around 12 percent of Syrians were members of the Alawite sect—an ethno-religious group with loose ties to Shi'ism. Even though the Alawites were a minority group, the ruling Assad family and most senior members of the regime's security apparatus came from this demographic. Other religious groups included the Christians and the Druze, which together made up about 15 percent of the population. Kurds accounted for 7 to 15 percent of Syrians (*Map 4*).[13]

When civil war broke out in Syria in the wake of the 2011 Arab Spring protests against the corrupt, repressive Assad regime, long-suppressed religious and ethnic grievances came to the surface. The insurgent forces opposed to the Syrian government were largely Sunni and Arab, in keeping with the country's demographics. As the Syrian military enjoyed extensive support from the Shi'a Iranian regime—and many of its personnel, especially in its officer corps, came from minority communities like the Alawites—the war took on a sectarian tinge. Would-be jihadists whose predecessors had gone to Iraq now traveled to Syria to take part in what they regarded as a new phase in a historical struggle between Sunnis and Shi'as.[14]

Opposition forces in Syria never coalesced into a single monolithic group. Instead, they splintered into independent factions and militias, each with its own ideological, religious, and ethnic character—and, in many cases, its own foreign sponsors. One of the largest groups, established in 2011 by defectors from the Syrian armed forces, was the Free Syrian Army, a loose confederation of hundreds of opposition "brigades" and "battalions." Though the group's members nominally shared the goal of bringing down the Assad regime, they only occasionally coordinated their efforts in pursuit of larger objectives.[15] Another notable faction, the Syrian Kurds, organized politically around the Democratic Union Party (Partiya Yekîtiya Demokrat; PYD) and formed militias called People's Protection Units (Yekîneyên Parastina Gel; YPG). These Kurdish forces pursued a policy of armed neutrality, avoiding overt action against the regime. The PYD's goals for greater Kurdish regional autonomy received a significant boost when the Syrian government withdrew most of

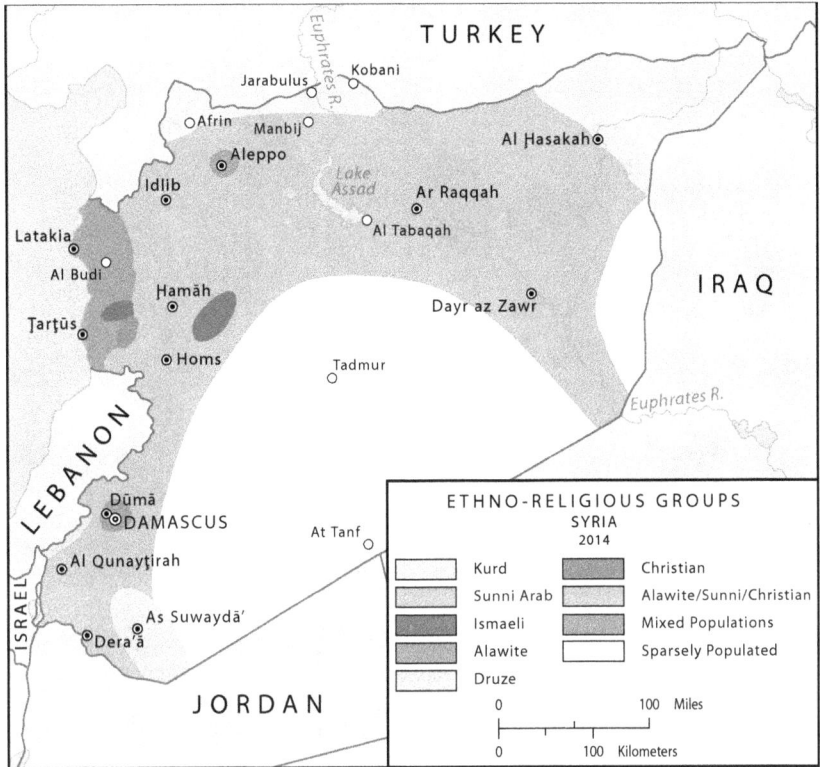

Map 4

its forces from the east in order to concentrate on the defense of the regime's heartland near the Mediterranean coast. Yet even as the PYD sought to establish an autonomous administration in the Kurdish areas of northern Syria, the lack of central state authority in the region left the border with Iraq largely unguarded and created a power vacuum that opposition groups could readily exploit.[16]

These developments gave new life to AQI. Following its near extinction in 2010, the group temporarily curtailed operations while it reconstituted under a new leader, the religious scholar Abu Bakr al-Baghdadi. By early 2011, it had recovered sufficiently to launch a renewed insurgency.[17] Recognizing the opportunity created by the chaos in Syria, AQI also dispatched several senior leaders across the border to organize a Syrian affiliate in August 2011.[18] This new group, known as Jabhat al-Nusra (the Support Front), was AQI's first inroad into the Syrian conflict. Al-Nusra positioned itself to absorb many of the foreign

13

Deputy Secretary of Defense Ashton B. Carter meets with Iraqi Prime Minister Nouri al-Maliki during a visit to Baghdad, 18 October 2012. *(Department of Defense)*

jihadists traveling to Syria to fight against the Assad regime. Its ranks also included several hundred veteran insurgents that the Syrian regime had released from its prisons after an amnesty in early 2011. By distancing itself from the indiscriminate violence characteristic of its parent organization and focusing on its opposition to the Syrian government, al-Nusra quickly became a popular and effective participant in Syria's factionalized opposition movement.[19]

Building on its successes in Syria, AQI launched a major new offensive in Iraq in July 2012.[20] Over the next year, it carried out waves of coordinated bombing attacks using vehicle-borne improvised explosive devices (VBIEDs). AQI also attacked Iraqi prisons, freeing hundreds of experienced insurgent fighters—many of whom had been detained by U.S. forces years before. Large numbers of these liberated insurgents joined AQI's ranks, adding to the group's resources and expertise.[21] By 2013, AQI had reclaimed its position as one of the most dangerous terrorist organizations in the world.

The spring of 2013 marked a new stage in AQI's campaign. In March, al-Nusra fighters participated in the capture of the

Syrian provincial capital of Ar Raqqah. This was one of the most important opposition victories up to that point, and it underscored the Assad regime's weakness. The following month, AQI unilaterally announced that it was merging with Jabhat al-Nusra to form a new organization, the Islamic State of Iraq and Syria. Although al-Nusra's leadership rejected the merger, instead pledging allegiance to the root al-Qaeda organization based in Pakistan, many of the group's fighters flocked to join ISIS. By the summer, ISIS was an established and rapidly growing presence in Syria. Seizing ground mainly from other opposition groups, it carved out a territory that it could use as a secure base for its operations in Iraq—including a new offensive against the ISF, which it launched in July.[22]

The Iraqi government's poor handling of intersectarian relations during the previous two years had created an ideal environment for the Islamic State's expansion. After the U.S. withdrawal, al-Maliki's treatment of Sunnis became increasingly heavy-handed. His government purged several leading Sunni politicians on spurious charges, culminating in the attempted arrest of Iraqi finance minister Rafi al-Issawi in December 2012. A Sunni protest movement emerged almost overnight, with large protest camps springing up in Sunni-majority cities. The government's decision to surround the camps with troops only made matters worse, and in January 2013 demonstrators fought Iraqi soldiers in the first of multiple clashes. In April, the ISF killed around forty Sunni protesters in Al Hawijah. As outraged Sunnis took up arms against the government, violence approached levels not seen since the height of the insurgency.[23]

The unrest created a combustible situation that ISIS turned to its advantage. In December 2013, Islamic State militants in western Al Anbar Province ambushed and killed the commander of the 7th Iraqi Army Division.[24] Days later, Prime Minister al-Maliki directed security forces to dismantle the Sunni protest camps in Ar Ramadi and Al Fallujah. The destruction of the camps, coupled with the arrest of a prominent Sunni lawmaker, Ahmed al-Alwani, set off a large-scale revolt. On 2 January 2014, Sunni rebels attacked Al Fallujah and Ar Ramadi with assistance from ISIS.[25] On the following day, ISIS announced the establishment of an "Islamic emirate" in Al Fallujah.[26] Although Iraqi forces regained control of Ar Ramadi within weeks, Al Fallujah remained in rebel hands. ISIS quickly assumed leadership over the insurgency.[27]

Abu Bakr al-Baghdadi in 2014 (*Department of State*)

At the same time, the Islamic State consolidated its position in Syria. On 13 January, ISIS seized full control of Ar Raqqah and made the city its capital. The border between Iraq and Syria effectively ceased to exist as eastern Syria and western Iraq became a unified territorial entity and theater of military operations, with ISIS forces traveling freely between the two countries.[28] In an audio statement released on 21 January, al-Baghdadi exhorted his fighters to continue their offensive against the Iraqi government, driving toward Baghdad and the Shi'a heartland in the south. He also looked farther afield, issuing a direct challenge to the United States: "Our last message is for the Americans. Soon we will be in direct confrontation, and the sons of Islam have prepared for such a day. So watch, for we are with you, watching."[29]

THE UNITED STATES INTERVENES

With Al Fallujah under the Islamic State's control, the insurgency against the Iraqi government entered a new and more dangerous phase. The ISF's failure to counter the lightly armed and outnumbered rebel militias raised questions about their military effectiveness, and forced the United States to reappraise its existing security assistance programs. It also raised the specter of a new "war in Iraq." As of January 2014, American assistance to the Iraqi military remained at a low level. Commanded since April 2013 by Lt. Gen. John M. Bednarek, OSC-I had undergone a series of personnel reductions that curtailed its already limited activities just as the security situation in Iraq reached a crisis point. Eliminated functions included support for Iraqi military leader development, professional military education, and senior staff training.[30] OSC-I also reduced the number of U.S.-run training sites from ten to three—ostensibly because it needed fewer sites to train the Iraqi military for conventional, as opposed to counterinsurgency, operations.[31] As the Sunni insurgency expanded, it became clear that this degree of support was insufficient.

Beginning in late 2013, the Iraqi government requested expanded American aid in the form of intelligence sharing and military hardware.[32] Prime Minister al-Maliki used a visit to Washington, D.C., in November 2013—his first since the U.S. withdrawal—to solicit additional U.S. military support. The United States agreed to provide limited aid, and an initial shipment of Hellfire air-to-ground missiles arrived on 19 December.[33] The Iraqis employed these munitions against ISIS camps and staging areas in Al Anbar Province.[34] To enhance the Iraqi military's surveillance capabilities, the United States also promised to supply ten Scan Eagle surveillance unmanned aerial vehicles (UAVs) and forty-eight Raven UAVs.[35] Meanwhile, OSC-I personnel began to advise the Iraqis more directly.[36] Al-Maliki even suggested that Americans might resume training the ISF on a large scale, possibly using facilities in Jordan.[37]

The prospect of a more extensive commitment of American ground forces nevertheless remained remote. For the Obama administration, the withdrawal in 2011 had been a key foreign policy achievement, marking the end of a long, bloody, and unpopular war. After the fall of Al Fallujah, Secretary of State John F. Kerry took pains to stress that the United States would not be returning to Iraq. Stating that the conflict in Iraq "belongs to the Iraqis," he affirmed that "we're not contemplating putting boots on the ground."[38] Meanwhile, al-Maliki was equally adamant that he saw no need for the United States to send troops because Iraq had "a strong army."[39]

By late spring of 2014, however, both sides' objections to a renewed U.S. commitment seemed less compelling. The turning point came when ISIS launched a major assault on the city of Mosul in early June. The forces guarding the city included two Iraqi Army divisions with an official combined strength of

25,000 troops, while ISIS's attack force consisted of about 1,500 militants. Yet the disparity between the two forces was not as severe as it appeared to be on paper. Iraqi Army officers routinely overreported the actual number of troops in their units and pocketed the unclaimed pay for their nonexistent "ghost soldiers." Because of this systemic corruption, one of the brigades defending Mosul contained only one-fifth of its reported personnel.[40] The Iraqi divisions also dispersed their soldiers in small checkpoints throughout the city, limiting their ability to meet a conventional attack. These factors made it possible for ISIS to overrun Mosul in a matter of days. By 10 June, the two defending divisions had disintegrated as the Iraqi soldiers discarded their weapons and uniforms and fled. At a stroke, the Islamic State found itself in control of Iraq's third-largest city.[41]

Three days later, President Obama publicly addressed the fall of Mosul and outlined an initial response. Though the United States would not undertake renewed combat operations in Iraq, American forces would step up their assistance to the Iraqi military to forestall a further collapse. He announced that around 300 special operations soldiers would deploy to "assess how we can best train, advise, and support Iraqi security forces going forward."[42] Fighting ISIS was not to be part of their mission. The president imposed a strict limit on the total number of U.S. troops on the ground and mandated restrictive rules of engagement, forbidding American forces from engaging the enemy except in self-defense.[43] At the same time, the White House also took steps to protect the numerous U.S. citizens already in Iraq. A 275-person military contingent, consisting of CENTCOM's Crisis Response Force and a U.S. Navy Fleet Antiterrorism Security Team platoon, deployed to Baghdad to bolster the defenses of the U.S. embassy, beginning on 14 June. These units would be the first American combat troops committed to Iraq in more than two years.[44]

At that time, ISIS's advance showed no sign of slowing. On 11 June, its fighters pushed south into Salah ad Din Province, capturing Bayji and besieging the nearby oil refinery. By nightfall, militants had taken control of Tikrit—229 kilometers south of Mosul.[45] The next day, ISIS forces massacred 1,700 captured Iraqi military personnel—mostly Iraqi Air Force Academy cadets—at the nearby Camp Speicher, and clashed with Iraqi troops outside of Samarra' just over an hour's drive from Baghdad.[46] The outlook in the Iraqi capital was dire. By the end of June, ISIS had rendered the equivalent of about five divisions combat ineffective, and defeatism plagued the Iraqi high command.[47] As one U.S. officer later recalled, senior Iraqi leaders after the fall of Mosul "seemed to be lacking in confidence. Most of the Iraqi generals could not even look me in the eye. . . . ISIS seemed unstoppable to them."[48] In northern Iraq, the ISF had virtually ceased to exist, and the Peshmerga, the military forces of Iraq's autonomous Kurdistan Regional Government (KRG), moved forward to fill the vacuum.[49] Even with the Kurdish presence in the area, however, large parts of northern Iraq remained undefended. Flush with victory, ISIS proclaimed the establishment of a new "caliphate"—a theocratic state that encompassed, in theory, all Muslims throughout the world—at the end of June (*Map 5*).[50]

Against this backdrop of military catastrophe for the Iraqi state, the White House hastily established a command-and-control construct and legal framework for an American intervention in Iraq. On 23 June, the United States and the Iraqi Ministry of Foreign Affairs exchanged diplomatic notes guaranteeing legal immunity for American forces in the country, a necessary condition for the sustained deployment of U.S. troops.[51] The next day, CENTCOM designated Lt. Gen. James L. Terry's U.S. Army Central (ARCENT) as Joint Forces Land Component Command–Iraq (JFLCC-I), assigning the South Carolina–based headquarters responsibility for directing American ground operations against ISIS.[52] Along with its new mission, ARCENT would continue to perform its standing role as the administrative headquarters for U.S. Army units throughout the Middle East. CENTCOM designated Iraq and Syria as the joint operations area for JFLCC-I, part of a wider theater of operations encompassing Jordan and the nations of the Gulf Cooperation Council.[53]

Although JFLCC-I provided overall direction for the U.S. ground forces in Iraq, General Terry delegated considerable authority to the ARCENT deputy commander, Maj. Gen. Dana J. H. Pittard, placing all of the conventional U.S. ground forces in Iraq under his direct command. Pittard arrived in Baghdad on 24 June at the head of a one-hundred-person headquarters element, which he used to establish a joint operations center in the U.S. embassy compound. The center served as a forward headquarters for the American ground forces in Iraq and enabled closer coordination with the Iraqi high command.[54]

Pittard also attached a small team to the Iraqi Combined Joint Operations Command in the Ministry of Defense to serve

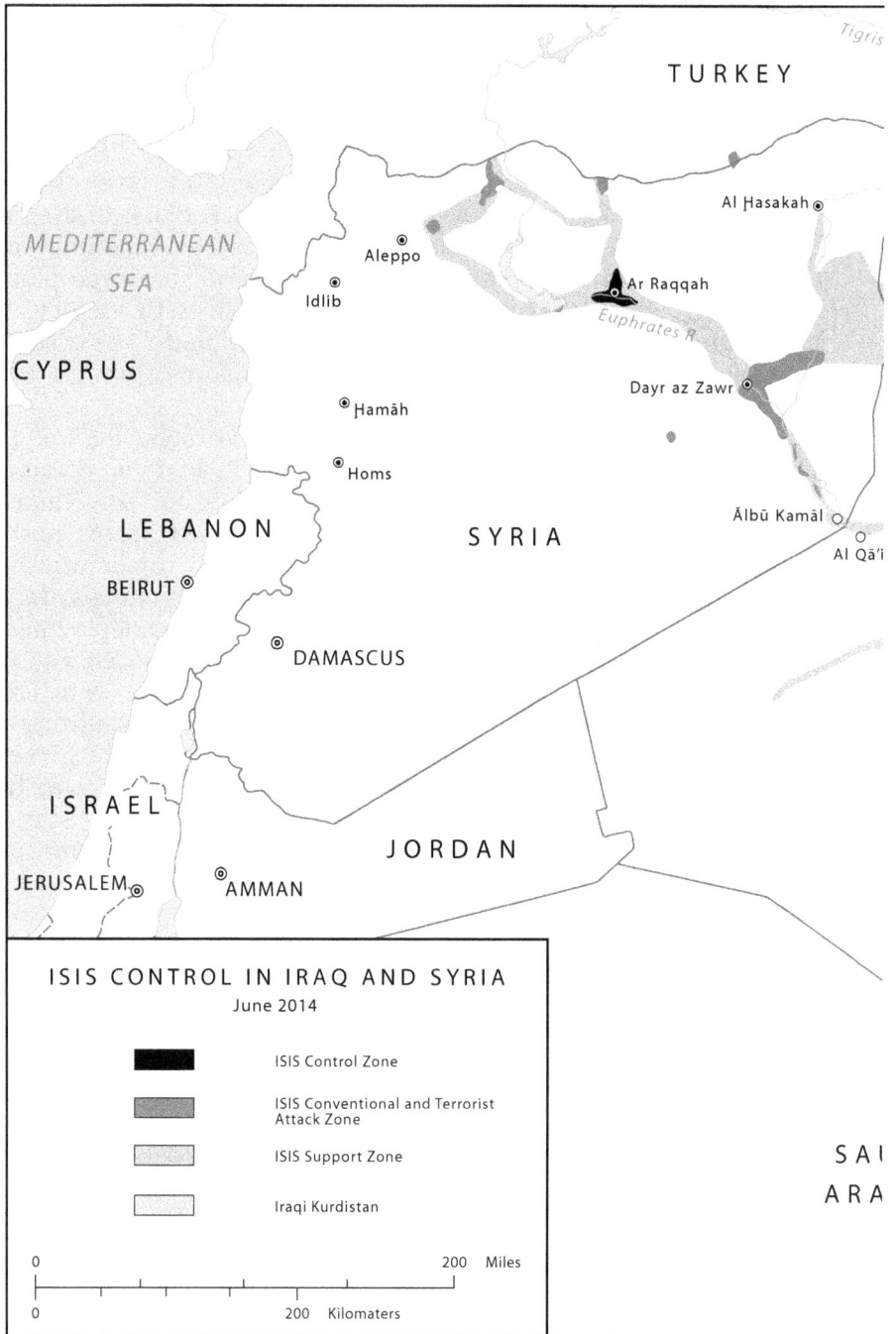

TURKEY

Tigris

MEDITERRANEAN
SEA

Al Ḥasakah ⊙

Aleppo ⊙

Idlib ⊙

⬤ Ar Raqqah

Euphrates R.

CYPRUS

Dayr az Zawr ⊙

⊙ Ḥamāh

⊙ Homs

Ālbū Kamāl ⊙

LEBANON

SYRIA

Al Qā'i ○

BEIRUT ⊙

⊙ DAMASCUS

ISRAEL

JORDAN

JERUSALEM ⊙

⊙ AMMAN

ISIS CONTROL IN IRAQ AND SYRIA
June 2014

ISIS Control Zone

ISIS Conventional and Terrorist
Attack Zone

ISIS Support Zone

Iraqi Kurdistan

| 0 | | | | | 200 | Miles |

| 0 | | 200 | Kilomaters |

SA|
ARA

Map 5

20

Sinjār

Mosul

Erbil

IRAN

Kirkūk

Bayjī

Rāwah

Tikrīt

Sāmarrā'

Ḥadīthah

Ba'qūbah

Hīt

Ar Ramādī

Al Fallūjah

BAGHDAD

IRAQ

Tigris R

An Najaf

Euphrates R

Al Baṣrah

ŞAUDI
ARABIA

KUWAIT

as permanent liaisons with ISF senior leadership. A second joint operations center later opened in Erbil, where it performed a similar function with the KRG and Peshmerga.[55]

Among General Pittard's first tasks on his arrival in Baghdad was to support the 300 special operations troops that President Obama had dispatched to assess the ISF. Grouped into six teams, they fanned out from Baghdad beginning on 24 June and visited nearby Iraqi units down to the brigade level. Their findings—which evaluated a range of factors, including equipment, morale, and leadership—were generally disappointing. The teams' final report, completed in two weeks, concluded that the Iraqi military suffered from significant weaknesses and required extensive retraining and reorganization. It also noted that many Iraqi units had been infiltrated by Iranian-backed Shi'a militias and therefore were unreliable.[56]

Fortunately, the threat to Baghdad itself subsided by early July. Days after the fall of Mosul, a prominent Iraqi Shi'a cleric, Grand Ayatollah Ali al-Sistani, had called for volunteers to defend the capital and guard Shi'a holy sites. In response, almost 100,000 fighters flocked to Baghdad, where the Iraqi government recognized them officially as the Popular Mobilization Forces (PMF). Arrayed alongside the remnants of the regular ISF, the PMF ensured that an attack on the capital would be unlikely to succeed.[57] The American attitude toward these volunteers, however, was ambivalent at best. It quickly became apparent that the PMF drew most of its fighting force from Shi'a militia groups, some of which had committed atrocities against Sunnis during Iraq's civil war. Moreover, the PMF aligned itself explicitly with Iran and its Shi'a leadership, and an Iranian military officer—Maj. Gen. Qassem Soleimani, the head of the Islamic Revolutionary Guard Corps' elite Quds Force—positioned himself as one of the PMF's key backers.[58] The PMF's potential combat power was significant, but U.S. officials feared that it ultimately might be directed against Iraqi civilians, not just against ISIS.

In the short term, the combined forces of the PMF and the ISF protected the northern approaches to Baghdad, but ISIS's offensive momentum was not yet spent. After defeating an Iraqi counterattack on Tikrit in July, the Islamic State resumed its advance at the beginning of August, moving on several objectives in the north.[59] Included among these was the Mosul Dam, located on the Tigris River about 35 kilometers northwest of Mosul. Coming under attack early in the month, the troops defending the facility held out for about a week before withdrawing on

7 August, leaving it in ISIS's hands.[60] At the same time, the Islamic State began to approach the Kurdish capital at Erbil, reaching a point only 35 kilometers from the city by 6 August.[61] Finally, ISIS launched an offensive against the Yazidis—a minority group that lived in the countryside west of Mosul. Fleeing the Islamic State's onslaught, tens of thousands of Yazidis sought refuge on Mount Sinjar, a cigar-shaped elevation near the Syrian border. For the Iraqis and the Americans, the situation was spiraling out of control.[62]

These developments demanded a direct response. On the evening of 7 August, President Obama addressed the nation on the Iraq crisis once again—this time to announce that he had authorized U.S. forces to launch targeted airstrikes against the Islamic State. "When we have the unique capabilities to help avert a massacre," he explained, "then I believe the United States of America cannot turn a blind eye. We can act, carefully and responsibly, to prevent a potential act of genocide."[63]

OPERATIONS

Around 1345 on 8 August 2014, a pair of American F/A–18 Hornet fighter jets dropped multiple 500-pound GBU–54 laser-guided bombs on an ISIS mobile artillery piece shelling Kurdish positions near Erbil. Several hours later, American F/A–18s and remotely piloted aircraft destroyed an ISIS convoy and mortar position. With these strikes, the United States entered into direct conflict with the Islamic State.[64]

CONTAINING ISIS, AUGUST 2014

Over the following days, the air campaign intensified. On 9 August, U.S. aircraft continued to bomb ISIS forces approaching the western outskirts of Erbil. At the same time, F–16C Fighting Falcon fighter jets hit several ISIS targets near Mount Sinjar, helping to relieve the pressure on the approximately 40,000 Yazidis besieged on the exposed mountaintop.[65] Cargo planes also began to deliver humanitarian aid, including food, water, and medical supplies, to the refugees on Mount Sinjar.[66] These measures had an immediate impact. The threat to Erbil disappeared within days, as ISIS realized that U.S. forces could easily detect—and destroy—any movement toward the Kurdish capital. Likewise,

Tech. Sgt. Lynn Morelly of the 816th Expeditionary Airlift Squadron delivers a humanitarian airdrop of food and water to displaced persons at Sinjar, Iraq, 9 August 2014. (*U.S. Air Force*)

airstrikes and humanitarian airdrops near Sinjar bought time for the Yazidis, who evacuated the Sinjar area at the rate of 2,000 people per day, beginning on 8 August. By 14 August, the Sinjar crisis was under control. Although ISIS still occupied the surrounding area, the few thousand refugees remaining on the mountain were safe and adequately provisioned.[67]

With Erbil secure and the threat of massacre averted, the next American priority was the recapture of the Mosul Dam. The U.S. military leadership feared that ISIS planned to destroy the facility, which would send an 8- to 26-meter-tall wave down the Tigris. Many Iraqi population centers lay on the banks of that river, including Baghdad. More than six million people potentially would be affected by flooding, with more than 500,000 at risk of being killed within a matter of days.[68]

On 16 August, American B–1B Lancer heavy bombers and F/A–18 Hornets carried out a series of airstrikes throughout northern Iraq in preparation for a counterattack to retake the Mosul Dam. The ground assault began the following morning, with an Iraqi Counter Terrorism Service (CTS) element attacking southwest toward the facility in concert with Kurdish forces. By

U.S. Navy F–18E Super Hornets supporting operations against ISIS, 4 October 2014. *(U.S. Air Force)*

the end of the day, the Iraqis had advanced roughly 24 kilometers and partially encircled the dam. The operation resumed on 18 August, with the Iraqi force assaulting and clearing the facility by nightfall with heavy U.S. air support.[69]

Another crisis arose less than a week later. On 23 August, the United Nations envoy in Iraq called for an international effort to relieve the Islamic State's siege of Amirli, a farming town 100 kilometers west of the Iranian border. Blockaded since June, Amirli's 15,000 inhabitants, most of whom were Shi'a Turkmen, were running out of supplies and required immediate support.[70] By 27 August, U.S. forces had completed plans for relief operations, in which ground forces would assault ISIS positions around the town from three directions. Kurdish troops would attack from the north, while an ISF element attacked from the south. Finally, Iranian-advised Shi'a militias—accompanied by a separate, Iranian-aligned Kurdish element—would attack from the east. The operation kicked off on 30 August and proceeded almost exactly as planned. With American air support, Iraqi forces entered Amirli by nightfall on 31 August, ending the six-week-long siege (*Map 6*).[71]

ESTABLISHING OPERATION INHERENT RESOLVE, SEPTEMBER–NOVEMBER 2014

By the end of August, the U.S. intervention had helped to contain the Islamic State's offensive, but the terrorist group remained an active threat. ISIS still held a massive area stretching from the eastern outskirts of Aleppo, in north-central Syria, to eastern Al Anbar Province in Iraq. Nearly the entire

TURKEY

SYRIA

Dahūk

Mosul
Dam

16–18 Aug

9–12 Aug

Mt. Sinjār

Mosul

Erbil
Airport

IRAN

Tall 'Afar

Sinjār

Erbil

Tigris R.

8 Aug

As Sulaymānīyah

Makhmūr

Kirkūk

Bayjī

Amirli
30–31 Aug

Euphrates R.

Tikrīt

Al Qā'im

Sāmarrā'

Khānaqīn

SIS'S NORTHERN OFFENSIVE
NORTHERN AND CENTRAL IRAQ
August 2014

Iraqi Kurdistan

Major Engagement

ISIS Attack

Ba'qūbah

Ar Ramādī

Al Fallūjah

BAGHDAD

Baghdad
International
Airport

Al Iskandarīyah

Tigris R.

0   100   Miles

0   100   Kilometers

Karbalā'

Al Kūt

Al Hillah

Map 6

Euphrates River from the Turkish border to Baghdad fell under
the Islamic State's control. The group also controlled the Tigris
River from Mosul to a point south of Tikrit. With between 20,000
and 31,500 fighters—reinforced by a steady stream of foreign
jihadists—and hundreds of millions of dollars in cash, the Islamic
State was more than capable of defending its new conquests.[72]
It was, as Secretary of Defense Charles T. Hagel commented,
"beyond a terrorist group." In Hagel's estimation, ISIS posed

"an imminent threat to every interest we have, whether it's in Iraq or anywhere else."[73] Although the airstrikes, humanitarian airdrops, and limited counterattacks that the United States had carried out or supported during the first month of operations in Iraq had been effective, they did not, on their own, constitute a strategy to defeat ISIS. Victory over the so-called caliphate would require a broader effort.

On 3 September, President Obama unveiled a campaign to "degrade and destroy" the Islamic State. He emphasized that this would be a long-term process. "Because of what's happened in the vacuum of Syria, as well as the battle-hardened elements of ISIS that grew out of al Qaeda in Iraq during the course of the Iraq war," he explained, "it's going to take time for us to be able to roll them back."[74] As the president elaborated one week later, U.S. forces would pursue four overlapping missions: an expanded campaign of airstrikes in support of Iraqi offensives; increased support for the Iraqi military in the form of training, intelligence sharing, and equipment; strengthened counterterrorism operations; and humanitarian assistance.[75]

The United States would also assemble an international coalition. On 13 September, President Obama appointed General (Ret.) John R. Allen, U.S. Marine Corps, as Special Presidential Envoy for the Global Coalition to Counter ISIL [ISIS].[76] Within a week, more than fifty nations, plus several international organizations, had joined the alliance. France and Great Britain both began airstrikes in Iraq by the end of the month.[77]

Underlying the move toward a greater commitment in Iraq was a major change in the country's political landscape. Many in the U.S. government blamed Iraqi Prime Minister al-Maliki for ISIS's expansion. As Secretary Kerry later observed, "Long-boiling sectarian resentments between Sunni and Shia found a violent synergy with weak, divisive leadership. Prime Minister Nouri al-Maliki clumsily helped create the environment that allowed for the rise of Daesh [ISIS] by consolidating power among the Shia elite instead of uniting Iraq." Convinced, in Kerry's words, that "you couldn't defeat Daesh [ISIS] with Maliki at the helm in Baghdad," the Obama administration worked behind the scenes to promote a transfer of power after the fall of Mosul.[78] Amid mounting pressure, al-Maliki finally resigned on 14 August, after more than eight years in office. President Obama welcomed al-Maliki's successor, Haider al-Abadi, as a more inclusive and nonsectarian alternative—a leader who would govern on behalf of all Iraqis, not just the country's Shi'a majority.[79]

27

As part of its new strategy, the Obama administration expanded operations against ISIS to encompass the group's territories in Syria. In early September, the president requested congressional authorization to train and equip "appropriately vetted elements" of the Syrian opposition as a proxy against the Islamic State.[80] Congress approved this request on 19 September, and Special Operations Command Central (SOCCENT) established a dedicated headquarters—Combined Joint Interagency Task Force–Syria (CJIATF-S)—to oversee the creation of a Syrian proxy force in early 2015. The SOCCENT commander, Maj. Gen. Michael K. Nagata, assumed responsibility for this effort.[81] Meanwhile, the coalition also began airstrikes against the Islamic State in Syria. On 22 September 2014, U.S. aircraft executed several strikes against ISIS and the al-Qaeda–affiliated Khorasan Group.[82] Five Arab states joined in the air campaign in Syria on the following day.[83]

Coalition operations in Syria took place in a diplomatic gray area. The Syrian government did not request assistance, and the United States made no attempt to cooperate with the Assad regime. President Obama had called for Bashar al-Assad to "step aside" as leader of Syria in the aftermath of the 2011 Arab Spring protests. In 2012, the United States recognized the rebel Syrian Opposition Council as the legitimate representatives of the Syrian people, having closed the American embassy in Damascus earlier that year.[84] Despite this breakdown in relations, al-Assad seemed to give tacit permission for the U.S. air campaign when he stated, after the first coalition airstrikes in Syria, that he welcomed "any international anti-terrorism effort." However, Syria retained a large air defense network—a latent threat to U.S. assets if the Assad regime ever chose to reject American involvement in the region.[85]

As the campaign against the Islamic State evolved in September, the military commands tasked with fighting the terrorist group underwent a broad reorganization. With non-U.S. forces engaged in ground operations, JFLCC-I became a multinational headquarters, the Combined Forces Land Component Command–Iraq (CFLCC-I), on 17 September. In October, a detachment from Maj. Gen. Paul E. Funk II's 1st Infantry Division assumed responsibility for CFLCC-I and relieved General Pittard's staff in Erbil and Baghdad.[86] The U.S. Department of Defense also formalized the campaign against ISIS as an overseas contingency operation, designated Operation INHERENT RESOLVE, on 17 October. The name, chosen

Army Lt. Gen. James L. Terry, commander of Combined Joint Task Force–Operation INHERENT RESOLVE (CJTF-OIR), briefs the press on operations in Iraq, 18 December 2014. *(Department of Defense)*

after some debate in the Pentagon, reflected the coalition's "deep, unwavering commitment to permanently defeat ISIS through the integrated use of all instruments of national power."[87]

To oversee operations against ISIS, CENTCOM directed General Terry to establish a dedicated joint and multinational task force, Combined Joint Task Force–Operation INHERENT RESOLVE. Terry would be "dual hatted," simultaneously heading both his original headquarters and CJTF-OIR—although he delegated the day-to-day leadership of ARCENT to his deputy, General Pittard. The staffs of both commands overlapped considerably, a dynamic that caused some strain for ARCENT's overstretched personnel.[88]

Based out of Camp Arifjan, Kuwait, the new combined joint task force exercised operational or tactical control over two main entities: a land component command (CFLCC-I)—and a special operations command, Special Operations Joint Task Force–Iraq (SOJTF-I). The 1st Theater Sustainment Command also fell under CJTF-OIR's operational control, providing logistical support. At the same time, several U.S. and coalition elements supporting OIR remained independent of the new headquarters. The coalition's air component command, a separate special operations task force based in northern Iraq, and CJIATF-S all

29

reported directly to CENTCOM. Finally, OSC-I remained under the U.S. Department of State.[89]

Many, but not all, of the military tasks associated with the conflict with the Islamic State fell under CJTF-OIR's control. In the first place, CFLCC-I was primarily responsible for training and equipping the ISF (*Map 7*). Beginning in late 2014, General Funk established four training sites where U.S. troops worked with nine ISF and three Peshmerga brigades. These units then served as the foundation of four reconstituted Iraqi Army divisions—the 6th, 7th, 15th, and 16th. At the same time, SOTJF-I also contributed to the training mission, instructing CTS forces and helping to organize Sunni tribal militias.[90] Additionally, both CJTF-OIR's ground forces and special operations commands advised ISF units engaged in combat operations. CFLCC-I embedded advisers with high-level Iraqi headquarters, and the U.S. contingents training Iraqi and Kurdish forces advised nearby ISF formations down to the division level. Meanwhile, SOJTF-I advised CTS brigades and battalions, and even accompanied Iraqi units on a limited basis.[91]

Responsibility for conducting the air campaign was more diffuse. All coalition aircraft in the Middle East fell under the control of U.S. Air Forces Central's Combined Air Operations Center, located in Qatar. At the same time, several different strike cells—not all of which reported to General Terry's headquarters—identified and approved targets for these aircraft. CJTF-OIR's subordinate commands operated strike cells that coordinated close air support to Iraqi units. CENTCOM's air component command also conducted its own bombing missions deep within ISIS territory, targeting the group's infrastructure, resources, forces, and leaders.[92]

DEGRADING ISIS, 2014–2015

Coalition planners conceived of OIR as a three-phase campaign. During the first phase, the Iraqis would remain on the strategic defensive as coalition air strikes degraded the Islamic State and halted its advance. At the same time, coalition ground forces would train and equip new ISF and Peshmerga brigades. With the terrorist group weakened and new Iraqi units taking the field, the campaign would then enter its second phase. This would involve a counteroffensive to isolate and liberate the caliphate's main strategic assets in Iraq, most importantly Mosul. By the end of this stage of the operation, ISIS would be

COALITION TRAINING SITES
NORTHERN AND CENTRAL IRAQ
2014–2015

Iraqi Kurdistan

| 0 | | 100 | Miles |
| 0 | | 100 | Kilometers |

TURKEY

SYRIA

IRAN

Dahūk

Mosul Dam

Mt. Sinjār

Sinjār

Tall 'Afar

Mosul

Erbil Airport

Erbil

Tigris R.

Makhmūr

As Sulaymānīyah

Kirkūk

Bayjī

Amirlī

Tikrīt

Al Qā'im

Sāmarrā'

Khānaqīn

Ḩadīthah

Euphrates R.

Al Baghdādī

Al Asad Air Base

Camp Taji

Ba'qūbah

Ar Ramādī

Al Fallūjah

Al Taqaddum Air Base

BAGHDAD

Besmaya

Baghdad International Airport

Al Iskandarīyah

Karbalā'

Tigris R.

Al Kūt

Al Ḩillah

Map 7

expelled from all the major Iraqi population centers. The main
effort during the third and final phase would then shift to Syria,
where coalition-backed ground forces would destroy the last
remnants of the Islamic State. During this period, CJTF-OIR
would also work to stabilize liberated areas in order to forestall
a renewed insurgency.[93]

31

For its part, the Islamic State did not remain passively on the defensive. This became obvious in mid-September, when it launched a major assault on the Kurdish-majority town of Kobani ('Ayn al 'Arab) in northern Syria.[94] ISIS committed 4,000 militants to the operation—twice as many as had participated in the capture of Mosul in June—as well as numerous armored fighting vehicles, including multiple tanks. Its forces outnumbered and outgunned the YPG militia fighters defending the town. Thousands of civilians fled the area, seeking safety across the border in Turkey.[95]

The coalition responded quickly. On 27 September, the air campaign in Syria expanded to include strikes in support of the YPG in Kobani.[96] Although this effort diverted air power from the main effort in Iraq, it enabled the coalition to degrade ISIS's most experienced forces. As the head of CENTCOM, General Lloyd J. Austin III, explained in October, "The more I attrite him [ISIS] there [in Kobani], the less I have to fight him on some other part of the battlefield."[97] For four months, coalition aircraft rained munitions on ISIS positions, bolstering the Kurdish defenders and inflicting hundreds of casualties. American B–1B Lancers routinely expended their entire ammunition payloads during sorties. Coalition C–130 Hercules cargo planes also airdropped tons of supplies to the YPG.[98] This support enabled the Kurds to hold out against ISIS's onslaught and eventually to counterattack and recapture parts of the town. With losses mounting, the Islamic State finally abandoned its offensive in January 2015.[99]

The battle for Kobani was a major victory for both the coalition and the YPG. The Islamic State lost around 1,000 fighters, including many veterans.[100] Moreover, its bid to gain access to a key border crossing—a potential smuggling route for supplies and militants—ended in failure. Equally significant, the defeat dealt a blow to ISIS's aura of invincibility, showing that the caliphate could be beaten.[101] At the same time, the YPG demonstrated that it was capable of defeating the Islamic State—given sufficient U.S. air support. However, diplomatic considerations prevented the United States from providing more than minimal resources for the Syrian Kurds. The YPG had connections to Turkey's Kurdistan Workers' Party (Partîya Karkerên Kurdistanê; PKK), a militant Kurdish political group designated as a terrorist organization by the U.S. Department of State.[102] Open coalition alignment with the Kurdish militia, or even a deeper partnership, thus remained out of the question.

A U.S. Marine fires an MG42 medium machine gun while a Danish coalition member spots targets during live-fire training for CJTF-OIR forces at Al Asad Air Base, Iraq, 1 June 2015. *(U.S. Marine Corps)*

For the time being, the United States would continue its efforts to organize a new Syrian partner force from scratch.

While the battle for Kobani raged in Syria, CJTF-OIR set to work rebuilding the ISF. Two training sites opened before the end of 2014, with detachments from Col. Jason Q. Bohm's Special Purpose Marine Air Ground Task Force and the 2d Battalion, 34th Armored Regiment, of the 1st Brigade Combat Team, 1st Infantry Division, moving into Al Asad Air Base and Camp Taji, respectively.[103] A total of four Iraqi battalions reported for training at these facilities by January.[104] The first full-strength rotation of U.S. trainers, approximately 1,000 soldiers from Col. Curtis A. Buzzard's 3rd Brigade Combat Team, 82d Airborne Division, deployed early in the new year, taking over operations at Camp Taji and establishing a coalition presence at the Besmaya Range Complex.[105]

During the first half of 2015, the initially substantial American involvement in training Iraqi and Kurdish forces gradually decreased as other coalition members assumed primary responsibility for that mission.[106] Early in the year, a 200-person Spanish military element arrived in Iraq and took the lead in training the ISF at the Besmaya Range Complex, relieving Colonel Buzzard's paratroopers.[107] In March, the French military established its own training site near Baghdad.[108] Meanwhile, smaller international contingents formed partnerships with U.S. trainers—a Danish company, for example, teamed up with the marines at Al Asad.[109]

Throughout early 2015, the conflict in Iraq remained in balance. With coalition support, Iraqi and Kurdish forces made modest gains during the winter and early spring, but the Islamic State contested Salah ad Din Province and tightened its grip on Al Anbar.[110] Clashes near Al Asad Air Base even threatened to draw coalition ground troops into direct confrontation with the terrorist group.[111] After months of skirmishing, ISIS forces seized part of the village of Al Baghdadi on 12 February, approaching within 10 kilometers of the training facility.[112] The following day, a squad of well-armed militants, clad in Iraqi uniforms, attacked the base. Although the Iraqis defeated this incursion without direct support, the 300-person coalition detachment on site came perilously close to engaging in ground combat. The Iraqis soon recaptured the village, but ISIS forces remained nearby, bombarding Al Asad intermittently with artillery and 122-mm. rockets. In March, CFLCC-I deployed a U.S. Army M109A6 Paladin self-propelled howitzer platoon to the air base to provide counterbattery fire.[113]

Despite these signs of resilience, U.S. leaders were confident that ISIS was on the run.[114] On 3 March, General Austin testified before Congress that "our military campaign is having the desired effects," stating that the coalition had "halted ISIL's [ISIS's] advance in Iraq," and that "the enemy is now in a 'defensive crouch,' and is unable to conduct major operations and seize additional territory."[115] Apparent proof of this claim came just days later, when the Iraqi military and its supporting militias launched a major offensive to retake the city of Tikrit. Spearheaded by 20,000 Iranian-backed PMF fighters, the operation served as a test of the Iraqi government's ability to defeat the Islamic State without U.S. assistance. In this sense, it was a disappointment. By mid-March, the fighting had degenerated into a bloody stalemate, with ISIS killing between forty and sixty ISF soldiers or PMF fighters every day.[116] Hoping to regain momentum, Prime Minister al-Abadi formally requested U.S. air support, which President Obama promised to provide on the condition that the Iranian-backed militias withdrew from the city. Once the Iraqis met this demand, coalition airstrikes began on 25 March.[117] ISIS's resistance rapidly collapsed, and the Iraqis took control of the majority of the city by early April. The liberation of Tikrit, with its prewar population of 160,000, was by far the coalition's most significant victory over the Islamic State up to that point.

Unfortunately, reverses in Al Anbar Province overshadowed the victory in Tikrit and belied optimistic assessments of the progress of the campaign. On 15 May, ISIS militants launched a surprise attack on the provincial capital of Ar Ramadi. Assaults on ISF positions using armor-plated suicide vehicle-borne improvised explosive devices (SVBIEDs), accompanied by swift and brutal reprisals against civilians and captured military personnel, drove the ISF from the city in company with thousands of refugees. By 18 May, Ar Ramadi was entirely in the hands of the Islamic State.[118] ISIS followed up this success by advancing on Baghdad in the hopes of preempting an Iraqi counterattack.[119] At the same time, it scored a second major victory in Syria, capturing the city of Palmyra from the Assad regime on 20 May.[120] The terrorist group appeared to be on the brink of repeating—or surpassing—its victorious June 2014 offensive. By the end of the month, however, airstrikes, combined with the rapid redeployment of Shi'a militias and ISF units, had halted ISIS's advance toward Baghdad. In hindsight, the Islamic State's advance in May 2015 was the high-water mark of its war with the Iraqi government.[121]

The ISF's defeat at Ar Ramadi prompted a reappraisal of the coalition's efforts against the Islamic State. At President Obama's instigation, the National Security Council reviewed the campaign in late May. Its assessment noted that while the overall strategic framework of the counter-ISIS effort was adequate, its execution on the ground "can and should be strengthened."[122] In the short term, this meant that CJTF-OIR would shift focus from the Mosul counterattack to supporting Iraqi efforts to liberate the parts of Al Anbar under ISIS control, beginning with the provincial capital. To assist with this mission, an additional 450 U.S. troops—mainly marines from the II Marine Expeditionary Force—deployed to Al Taqaddum Air Base, less than 30 kilometers east of Ar Ramadi, where they would train and advise the 8th Iraqi Army Division and the Al Anbar Operations Command.[123] Overall command over U.S. ground forces fell to a 500-person element from the 82d Airborne Division, commanded by Maj. Gen. Richard D. Clarke, which relieved General Funk's 1st Infantry Division as Combined Joint Forces Land Component Command–Iraq (CJFLCC-I) headquarters—a modified designation for CFLCC-I, adopted earlier in the year—on 28 June.[124]

The campaign to liberate Ar Ramadi kicked off on 12 July. With heavy coalition air support, Iraqi forces made steady progress at first as they enveloped the provincial capital and demolished its surrounding obstacle belts. However, local ISIS counterattacks in late August blunted the offensive. With around 2,000 militants in the city, the Islamic State was able to conduct an active defense, launching frequent local attacks using SVBIEDs.[125] These suicide vehicles, along with the city's multilayered, explosives-laden defenses—not to mention the extreme temperatures, which often reached 120°F during the height of the summer—made forward movement difficult.[126]

With the offensive in Al Anbar Province temporarily stalled, both ARCENT and the 3d Brigade Combat Team, 82d Airborne Division, ended their OIR rotations in September. Col. Scott M. Naumann's 1st Brigade Combat Team, 10th Mountain Division, assumed responsibility for advising and training Iraqi forces on 17 September.[127] Five days later, the III Corps relieved ARCENT as CJTF-OIR headquarters.[128] Transitioning back to its standing role as CENTCOM's Army Service Component Command, ARCENT continued to provide logistical and administrative support for CJTF-OIR even after the end of its rotation.

In a little more than a year of active combat operations against the Islamic State, coalition forces had severely reduced the caliphate's territory, liberating 15,000 to 20,000 square kilometers of land in Iraq and 2,000 to 4,000 square kilometers in Syria.[129] CJTF-OIR had also inflicted heavy casualties on the terrorist group. In June 2015, the coalition estimated that at least 10,000 ISIS militants had been killed since the start of the campaign.[130] By mid-October, that figure had more than doubled.[131] Perhaps more significantly, the group's senior leadership also suffered heavy casualties. From the start of the U.S. air campaign in August 2014, coalition forces eliminated more than one hundred "high value individuals" and dozens of local ISIS leaders.[132]

The coalition's more constructive efforts to increase the capacity of its Iraqi and Kurdish partners also had borne fruit. By mid-October 2015, nearly 15,000 ISF and CTS personnel had completed training at coalition facilities. This achievement fell short of the intended training target of 24,000 soldiers, but it nevertheless substantially increased the combat strength of the Iraqi ground forces. Additionally, the Iraqi government mobilized almost 2,000 Sunni tribal fighters, with around 1,300 receiving training and equipment by early July.[133] Ultimately, ARCENT's tenure as CJTF headquarters laid the foundation for the coalition's victory over ISIS. It was, as the historian of a subsequent CJTF-OIR rotation noted, "a remarkable operational and [organizational] accomplishment."[134]

FROM AR RAMADI TO Q-WEST, 2015–2016

The III Corps, under Lt. Gen. Sean B. MacFarland, was well positioned to build on this foundation. Identified as ARCENT's relief in 2014, MacFarland's headquarters had ample time to prepare for its new assignment, conducting a series of command post exercises and tailoring its structure to the OIR mission requirements.[135] This advance planning was fortunate, as the III Corps' arrival in theater in September 2015 coincided with two developments that added greatly to the difficulty of the campaign.

The first of these was the failure of the New Syrian Forces, the U.S.-trained militia intended to serve as the coalition's partner in land operations in Syria. Interagency and special operations forces had begun training the militia's initial cohort at facilities in Turkey and Jordan in May 2015, and CJIATF-S under General Nagata had hoped to field 3,000 fighters by the end of the year. By July, however, the entire New Syrian Forces consisted of only about sixty men.[136] When the new militia deployed to Syria on 14 July, ISIS kidnapped two of its leaders and attacked the base camp of the Free Syrian Army faction that served as the group's recruiting pool. A second batch of seventy-one New Syrian Forces fighters proved little more effective when it entered Syria two months later. On 21 September, Jabhat al-Nusra militants forced the small contingent to surrender six pickup trucks and about one-quarter of its weapons and equipment.[137] President Obama suspended the New Syrian Forces training program on 9 October.[138]

The second major development was Russia's intervention in the Syrian civil war. Russia's military ties to Syria dated back to the 1950s, when the Syrian government aligned itself with the former Soviet Union. These ties continued even after the end of the Cold War. Russian President Vladimir V. Putin consequently watched with concern as the Syrian government, his one significant ally in the region, suffered a series of reverses that pushed it to the brink of outright defeat. He ultimately decided on a military response.[139] The Russians built up forces in Syria over the summer of 2015, before launching an air campaign against opponents of the Assad regime on 30 September.[140]

The Russian intervention made CJTF-OIR's task of defeating the Islamic State more difficult. The Russian forces in Syria largely ignored the areas controlled by ISIS, concentrating instead on assisting the Syrian government's efforts to reclaim the western part of the country, especially the city of Aleppo.[141] Included among the targets of these operations were Syrian opposition groups backed by the U.S.-led coalition.[142] On top of this direct threat to American interests, the presence of Russian aircraft in the airspace over Syria increased the possibility for accidental conflict between the two powers. By 2015, U.S.-Russian tensions were at dangerous levels. The United States had condemned the Russian annexation of the Crimean Peninsula in early 2014, as well as Putin's role in fomenting civil war in eastern Ukraine. In this strained political environment, the Obama administration definitively ruled out direct cooperation with the Russian effort in Syria, despite repeated Russian overtures for joint operations. As Secretary of Defense Ashton B. Carter later explained, such cooperation would undercut the United States' strategic position in the region, while "naively [granting] Russia an un-deserved leadership role in the Middle East."[143] Deteriorating relations with Russia continued to complicate the U.S. role in the region.

Within this context, the III Corps commenced a number of operational initiatives early in its rotation.[144] The first of these was the development of a new Syrian proxy to replace the New Syrian Forces. The YPG had thousands of experienced fighters and a preexisting territorial base in the Kurdish cantons in northern Syria. It also had a track record of success against the Islamic State, exemplified by its victory at Kobani. But the militia's connections to the PKK remained an obstacle. Moreover, as a Kurdish group, the YPG was far from an ideal choice to lead operations in ISIS's Syrian territories, which were inhabited predominantly by Sunni Arabs. In light of the ethnic tensions in the region, Ar Raqqah's population might see liberation by the Kurds as a kind of occupation. In early October, American special operations forces helped to resolve this dilemma by organizing several Arab militia groups into the Syrian Arab Coalition, which promptly affiliated itself with the YPG under the umbrella of another new group: the Syrian Democratic

Syrian President Bashar al-Assad meets with Russian President Vladimir Putin
to discuss military operations in Syria, 21 October 2015.
(Press Service of the President of Russia)

Forces (SDF).[145] The SDF issued a press release announcing its formation on 12 October. Less than twenty-four hours later, U.S. C–17 Globemaster cargo planes airdropped around fifty tons of ammunition to Syrian Arab Coalition units in northeast Syria.[146] By the end of the year, fifty American special operations advisers had deployed to support the Syrian Arab Coalition and other U.S.-aligned militias—the first sustained commitment of U.S. troops to Syria.[147]

The autumn also saw a major evolution in the coalition's air campaign. One of the Islamic State's primary sources of revenue was crude oil from Syria's Dayr as Zawr Province and Iraq's Ninawa Province. ISIS shipped thousands of barrels to the Turkish border every day and netted about $40 million per month from sales to smugglers.[148] Despite the importance of this trade to the caliphate's economy, the coalition had conducted only sporadic strikes on the terrorist group's oil infrastructure during the first fourteen months of combat operations. The coalition hesitated to attack oil-related targets because it lacked information on ISIS's oil production and sales network. However, a special operations raid on the home of ISIS's oil minister Abu Sayyaf in May 2015 provided the coalition with a detailed picture of how the Islamic State extracted, transported, and sold oil. This new intelligence enabled coalition planners to design an air campaign that could cripple a key pillar of ISIS's economy while minimizing civilian losses.[149]

After months of preparations, on 21 October CENTCOM's air component command commenced Operation TIDAL WAVE II—a reference to the Allies' strategic bombing campaign against Romanian oil refineries during World War II. Following a series of strikes on Syria's Al-Omar oil field, the operation expanded to include attacks on ISIS's fleet of tanker trucks, with four A–10 Thunderbolt II fighters and two AC–130 gunships destroying a total of 116 trucks in Dayr as Zawr Province on 16 November. Leaflets dropped by two F–15E fighters warned the drivers—most of whom were civilians—to flee before the first bombs landed.[150] These and subsequent attacks, which continued until late 2017, dealt considerable damage to ISIS's economic infrastructure. However, because the lion's share of the Islamic State's revenue came from taxes on the population of the areas it controlled, TIDAL WAVE II alone was not enough to destroy the caliphate's economy.[151]

Finally, the coalition adopted a much more aggressive approach to direct action missions by special operations forces. Coalition forces had already carried out several such raids in support of Operation INHERENT RESOLVE, including the Abu Sayyaf operation in May, but a new raiding policy unveiled in October 2015 enabled U.S. special operations personnel to take additional risks. As Secretary Carter informed Congress, "We won't hold back from supporting capable partners in opportunistic attacks against ISIL [ISIS] or conducting such missions directly."[152]

A tangible sign of this approach came less than a month after the III Corps' arrival. On 22 October, a group of thirty U.S. special operations troops accompanied a team of Kurdish commandos in an assault on an ISIS-operated prison in Al Hawijah. Militants had already killed eleven prisoners in the facility, and intelligence indicated that the terrorist group planned to execute seventy more, including seventeen Peshmerga fighters. Drone footage confirmed that ISIS militants had dug several mass graves for their victims nearby. Flown in before dawn by five American helicopters, the Kurdish commandos came under heavy fire after breaching the walled compound. Despite orders to support and observe the attack from the rear, two Americans rushed out of cover to aid the Kurds, and one—M. Sgt. Joshua L. Wheeler—died in the firefight. The U.S.-Kurdish force killed about twenty ISIS militants and captured a further five. They freed all seventy-five hostages but did not locate the Peshmerga soldiers believed to be held on site.[153]

Sergeant Wheeler was CJTF-OIR's second combat death. The first had taken place in March 2015, when a member of the Canadian Special Operations Regiment, Sgt. Andrew J. Doiron, fell to friendly fire.[154] These losses underscored the reality that coalition troops were in harm's way, even if they were fighting mainly through Iraqi and Syrian proxies.

While these new operational initiatives took effect, CJTF-OIR worked to jump-start the Iraqi offensive in Al Anbar. With encouragement from General MacFarland, Iraqi forces returned to the offensive at the beginning of October.[155] Within a week, the Iraqis had advanced 15 kilometers and completed their encirclement of Ar Ramadi, setting the conditions for the final assault on the city itself beginning on 25 November.[156] Progress during this phase was relatively swift. By 8 December, the ISF had liberated several neighborhoods in the southern part of the city and regained control of the Al Anbar Operations Command's headquarters. Iraqi forces also captured multiple Euphrates River bridges, which they used to reach ISIS's last remaining stronghold in central Ar Ramadi.[157]

After a third operational pause, during which airstrikes helped to defeat a major ISIS counterattack involving around fifteen SVBIEDs, Iraqi troops once again resumed their advance.[158] On 22 December, the ISF breached central Ar Ramadi, advancing from the south.[159] The Al Anbar provincial government complex fell by the end of the year, and Iraqi forces cleared out the last pockets of ISIS fighters by the end of March.[160] Sunni tribal fighters also deployed to the area to combat ISIS remnants and provide security.[161] The liberation of Ar Ramadi ultimately cost the Iraqis around 1,100 casualties, including 100 soldiers killed in action.[162] More than 600 ISIS fighters died during the campaign.[163]

This victory came on the heels of other coalition successes. In October, Iraqi CTS and Federal Police forces operating north of Baghdad secured the city of Bayji and its nearby oil refinery, ending more than a year of back-and-forth fighting.[164] Shortly after, the Peshmerga launched an assault to seize the city of Sinjar in concert with PKK and YPG militants, as well as local militias known as Sinjar Resistance Units. Kurdish fighters advancing to the south, down the slopes of Mount Sinjar, joined other elements moving in from the east and west along Highway 47. Rather than fighting and dying in place, as in Ar Ramadi, ISIS forces rapidly evacuated the city, leaving it in Kurdish hands by 13 November. The Kurdish fighters then fanned out through the surrounding villages, liberating much of the Sinjar area in less than a week.[165]

Finally, CJTF-OIR's new Syrian proxy, the SDF, opened its own offensive southwest of Kobani on 23 December. Within three days, the Syrian militia took control of a key regional asset: the Tishrin Dam. This facility produced about two-fifths of Syria's hydroelectric power, and also functioned as a bridge over the Euphrates.[166] Islamists had occupied the dam since November 2012, using it to transfer supplies between Ar Raqqah and Manbij, the only city on the Turkish-Syrian border still held by the Islamic State. Its loss left the ISIS contingent in Manbij isolated and open to attack.[167]

By the beginning of 2016, the campaign in Iraq was ready to proceed to its decisive phase—the liberation of Mosul.[168] The first tentative steps took place in early February, when the ISF's Ninawa Operations Command established a logistics base in the farming village of Makhmur, west of Erbil. Coalition forces arrived at the site beginning in February, with the 3d Battalion, 6th Field Artillery Regiment, overseeing initial construction. Military advisory teams arrived soon after.[169] These elements fell under the overall control of Maj. Gen. Gary J. Volesky's 101st Airborne Division, which assumed responsibility as Combined Joint Force Land Component Command—Operation INHERENT RESOLVE (CJFLCC-OIR) headquarters—the fourth and final designation for OIR's land component command—on 8 March.[170]

Other coalition forces also deployed in support of the upcoming offensive. In March, a battery of four M777A2 155-mm. howitzers from the 26th Marine Expeditionary Unit established a small firebase outside of Makhmur. The outpost quickly attracted ISIS's attention. On the morning of 19 March, Islamic State militants launched long-range Katyusha rockets against the base. Two missiles hit the facility—one landing harmlessly and the other exploding, wounding eight marines and killing a ninth, S. Sgt. Louis F. Cardin. Two days later, ISIS attacked the base with a squad-sized force. The marines easily defeated this ground assault, killing two of the enemy.[171] Despite this harassment, the battery was fully operational by the beginning of April, carrying out fire missions in support of nearby Iraqi forces on a daily basis.[172]

The first phase of the Mosul offensive, Operation VALLEY WOLF, began on 24 March.[173] Before the Iraqi forces could begin an assault on Mosul, they first would need to seize the city of Al Qayyarah and its nearby military airfield, Qayyarah Air Base West (known as "Q-West"), a little more than an hour's drive south of Mosul. Then, they would have to clear the 150-kilometer stretch of the Tigris River Valley between Al Qayyarah and Tikrit. Q-West Airfield was an elaborate facility that had served as a coalition forward operating base during Operation IRAQI FREEDOM, and the coalition intended to use it (rather than Makhmur) as the ISF's main staging area and logistics hub in northern Iraq.[174] Despite substantial coalition air support, the initial advance made only modest progress. Pushing west from Makhmur, the 15th Iraqi Army Division liberated several villages before ISIS snipers, improvised explosive devices (IEDs), and booby traps halted their advance. The Iraqi leadership paused Operation VALLEY WOLF in early April, with Q-West still out of reach.[175]

The ISIS forces in Ninawa, although weakened, could still execute complex offensive operations on a local level. On 3 May, the terrorist group launched a counterattack against Peshmerga positions outside of the village of Tal Asqaf, 32 kilometers north of Mosul. With 120 fighters and twenty armored vehicles, the ISIS contingent broke through the Kurdish front lines and reached the village, assaulting the Peshmerga units and an accompanying U.S. advisory team. In response, a coalition quick reaction force deployed and engaged the ISIS militants in a firefight that lasted throughout most of the day. By the time ISIS retreated, coalition forces had carried out thirty-one airstrikes, destroying numerous vehicles and killing fifty-eight ISIS militants. Kurdish losses were light, but one member of the coalition quick reaction force—MCPO Charles H. Keating IV— was mortally wounded in the battle.[176]

While the Iraqis clashed with ISIS in northern Iraq, the ISF continued its campaign to liberate Al Anbar. Having secured Ar Ramadi, the Iraqis pivoted east to Al Fallujah, which was

43

defended by an estimated 2,000 ISIS fighters.[177] In February, the ISF completely isolated the city, placing it under siege.[178] At the same time, the Iraqis massed troops northwest of Ar Ramadi for an assault on the city of Hit, liberating it by mid-April.[179] Finally, CTS units operating alongside the Al Anbar Police Special Tactics Battalion seized the town of Ar Rutbah in May, clearing one of the last remaining obstacles on the Baghdad-Amman highway—an overland trade route that was economically important for both Iraq and Jordan.[180]

The ISF launched its assault on Al Fallujah on 23 May. ISIS had prepared elaborate defenses during its two-and-a-half-year occupation of the city. An abundance of booby traps and IEDs, arrayed in several obstacle belts, made any advance difficult. Additionally, around 50,000 civilians—approximately one-fifth of the city's pre-ISIS population—remained in the area, raising concerns about collateral damage.[181] Despite these challenges, the operation made rapid progress. Spearheaded by CTS elements, Iraqi forces reached the outskirts of the city and broke into its southeastern district by the end of May.[182] Fighting during the following month was fierce, but the Iraqis cleared most of Al Fallujah's neighborhoods by 20 June.[183] One week later, around 1,000 ISIS fighters attempted to escape in two large convoys. Coalition surveillance assets identified the vehicles as hostile, however, and bombing runs by Iraqi and coalition aircraft on 28 and 29 June killed hundreds of militants.[184] The resulting devastation prompted comparisons to the "Highway of Death" in the 1991 Persian Gulf War, in which coalition airstrikes heavily damaged Iraqi military convoys retreating from Kuwait.[185] The Islamic State's defeat at Al Fallujah brought large-scale combat operations in eastern Al Anbar to a close. Much work remained, however, as the Iraqi government began reconstructing the region—an effort complicated by credible reports of atrocities committed by the PMF against Sunni Arab civilians.[186]

The Islamic State also tried to retaliate for its losses, albeit indirectly. Just days after the liberation of Al Fallujah, the terrorist group staged a suicide bombing that killed at least 292 civilians in a Shi'a neighborhood in central Baghdad.[187] The attack served as a reminder that the Islamic State could attack targets outside of its territory. ISIS also inspired terrorism farther afield. Unable to win on the battlefields of Iraq and Syria, it increasingly relied on terror attacks against civilians in Europe and the United States to boost its profile and entice new recruits. Throughout 2015 and 2016, attacks around the world—in Paris,

France; San Bernardino, California; Brussels, Belgium; Orlando, Florida; and Nice, France—inflicted hundreds of casualties and inspired widespread outrage.[188]

While the ISF liberated Al Anbar Province, the SDF encroached on the Islamic State's Syrian territory from multiple directions. In February, the Syrian militias captured Ash Shaddadah in eastern Syria, further constricting ISIS's supply lines into Iraq.[189] Early 2016 also saw the reappearance of the New Syrian Forces—rebranded by the coalition as the Vetted Syrian Opposition—after the group's disappointing debut in July and September 2015. In March, coalition special operations forces helped Vetted Syrian Opposition fighters capture At Tanf, a village located at the juncture of the Iraqi and Jordanian borders in southeastern Syria. This outpost, previously occupied by ISIS, would serve as a train-and-equip facility for the coalition-aligned fighters.[190] Meanwhile, President Obama authorized the deployment of an additional 250 special operations personnel to Syria in April, raising the size of the U.S. contingent in that country to 300.[191] With this support, the SDF resumed its advance toward Manbij in June. Led by the Syrian Arab Coalition, the SDF offensive made rapid progress and liberated the city by 12 August.[192]

Meanwhile, the summer saw the resumption of Operation VALLEY WOLF in northern Iraq (Map 8). On 18 June, two brigades from the Iraqi Army's 9th Armored Division departed Camp Speicher, outside of Tikrit, and advanced northwest along Highway 1. Swinging across the desert, the column pivoted and assaulted Q-West Airfield from the west, capturing the facility on 9 July. Less than a week later, the 15th Iraqi Army Division pushed west from Makhmur and executed an opposed river crossing over the Tigris River near Al Qayyarah, establishing a lodgment on the west bank. The two forces then linked up west of the Tigris.[193] In August, the Iraqi Army Bridge Regiment completed a pontoon bridge over the Tigris with support from the U.S. Army's 39th Engineer Battalion, enabling the transfer of supplies from Makhmur to the ISF's new logistics hub at Q-West. The 39th Engineer Battalion also cleared and reconstructed the airfield, which ISIS had laced with booby traps, and built a new headquarters facility for the ISF within forty-five days of the site's liberation.[194] Large numbers of coalition forces subsequently moved into Q-West, including a fresh deployment of 560 troops, drawn mainly from the 2d Brigade Combat Team, 101st Airborne Division.[195] The paratroopers joined a 1,239-person contingent from Col. Brett G. Sylvia's 2d Brigade Combat Team,

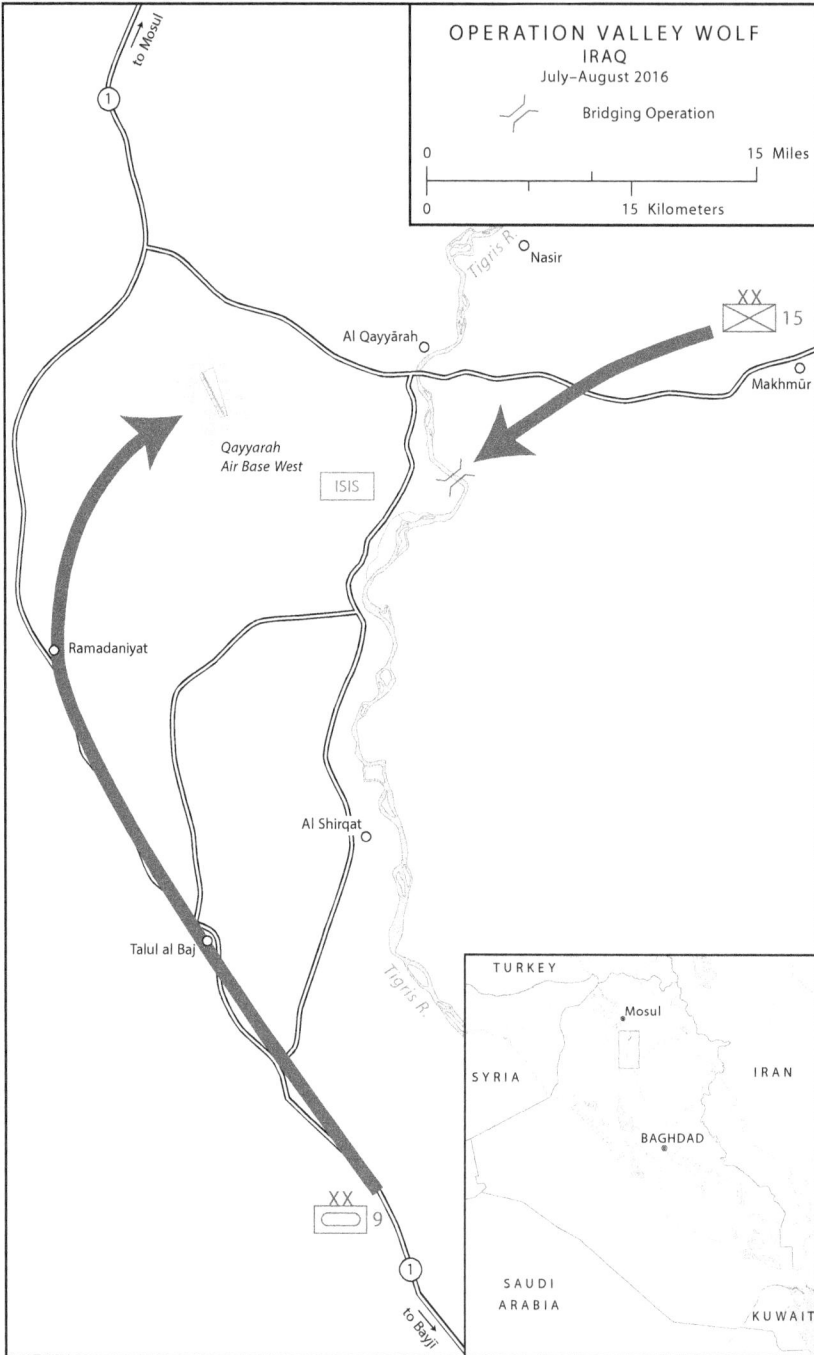

OPERATION VALLEY WOLF
IRAQ
July–August 2016

Bridging Operation

0   15 Miles

0   15 Kilometers

to Mosul

1

Tigris R.

Nasir

Al Qayyārah

XX
15

Makhmūr

Qayyarah
Air Base West

ISIS

Ramadaniyat

Al Shirqat

Tigris R.

Talul al Baj

XX
9

1

to Bayji

TURKEY

Mosul

SYRIA

IRAN

BAGHDAD

SAUDI
ARABIA

KUWAIT

Map 8

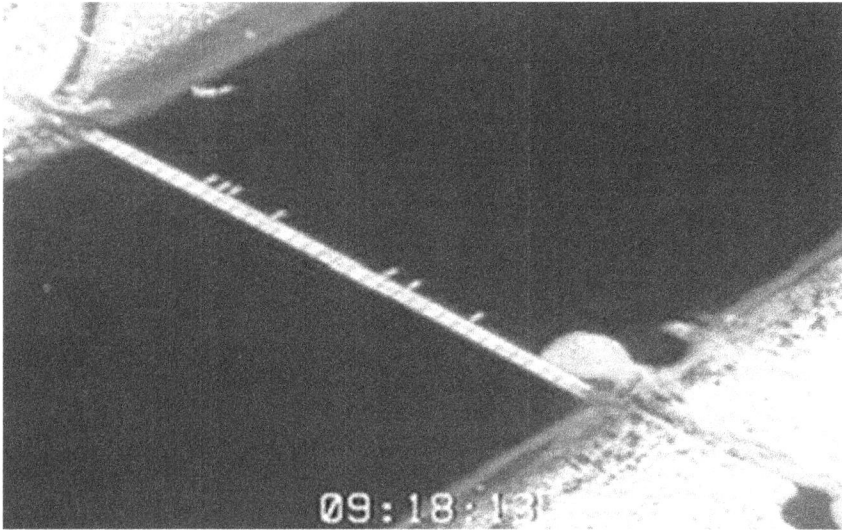

Remotely piloted aircraft footage of the completed bridge over the Tigris River, summer 2016. *(Combined Joint Task Force–Operation Inherent Resolve)*

101st Airborne Division, which had replaced Colonel Naumann's 1st Brigade Combat Team, 10th Mountain Division, as the primary U.S. training and advisory force in Iraq in May.[196]

The capture of Q-West and the bridging of the Tigris were among the last major operations overseen by the III Corps during its tenure as CJTF-OIR headquarters. On 21 August, General MacFarland transferred authority to the XVIII Airborne Corps under Lt. Gen. Stephen J. Townsend.[197] The campaign had progressed significantly during MacFarland's twelve months in command. The Iraqi military was much larger, better equipped, and more capable than it had been a year before. Around 6,000 Peshmerga militiamen and women and 20,000 tribal fighters, along with 12,696 Iraqi Army soldiers, 4,602 Iraqi Federal Police, and 1,665 CTS troops, had received training from coalition forces between August 2015 and August 2016. At the same time, ISIS's losses were significant, leaving the group without the capability to conduct major offensive operations in Iraq and Syria. During the same period, coalition forces and their Iraqi and Syrian partners had liberated around 14,000 square kilometers and had killed 24,345 ISIS militants.[198]

Despite these successes, however, the conflict was far from over. The Islamic State remained a dangerous opponent on the

47

defensive, with substantial resources and control over much of northern Iraq and eastern Syria. Moreover, its position in Mosul was well fortified, and the coalition expected ISIS's garrison of fanatical militants to defend their hold on the city to the bitter end.

Operation Eagle Strike: The Liberation of Mosul, 2016–2017

During the first weeks of its rotation, the XVIII Airborne Corps supported the Iraqi and Kurdish forces as they conducted shaping operations along the southern and eastern approaches to Mosul. The city of Al Qayyarah fell to the Iraqi military on 25 August, followed by Al Shirqat—the Islamic State's last outpost in Salah ad Din Province—a little under a month later. Meanwhile, the Peshmerga expanded its control over the countryside east of Mosul, liberating a dozen villages in mid-August.[199] For the most part, ISIS put up only token resistance as its fighters retreated to Mosul. In many villages, militants fled immediately after encountering Iraqi troops.[200]

Meanwhile, efforts to soften the Islamic State's defenses in Mosul also continued, with airstrikes destroying numerous targets, including a suspected chemical weapons manufacturing facility. At the same time, precision strikes continued to eliminate ISIS's high command. In July, coalition aircraft killed Abu Omar al-Shishani, one of the Islamic State's most capable field commanders. Another airstrike killed the terrorist group's chief spokesman, Abu Mohammad al-Adnani, in August.[201]

The Iraqi government finished its preparations for the Mosul offensive in October. At the beginning of the month, Prime Minister al-Abadi appointed Staff Lt. Gen. Abdul-Amir Rasheed Yarallah to head the operation, assigning three Iraqi Army divisions, one Federal Police division, a division-strength CTS task force (Task Force CTS), and the Federal Police's Emergency Response Division to his command. In total, the ISF massed approximately 65,000 military personnel to take part in the operation. General Yarallah also commanded more than 30,000 Peshmerga and Shi'a PMF troops, who would provide security and assist with isolating Mosul but would not take part in the attack on the city itself.

Opposing these 95,000 Iraqis and Kurds were between 3,000 and 5,000 ISIS militants holed up in the city, and a further 1,500 to 2,500 fighters within a ring of defensive outposts in the surrounding countryside. Split into three- to five-person teams

A U.S. Army M109A6 Paladin conducts a fire mission at Qayyarah West, Iraq, as the ISF push toward Mosul, 17 October 2016. *(U.S. Army)*

and equipped with an array of small arms and crew-served weapons, including heavy machine guns and mortars, these fighters constituted a skilled, well-armed, and highly motivated conventional force. But Mosul's defenders were also poised to make extensive use of unconventional capabilities. Many ISIS fighters went into battle wearing suicide vests. Others were responsible for driving the Islamic State's fleet of armored truck bombs.[202]

Mosul sprawled over a 227-square-kilometer area spanning both banks of the Tigris River. On the west bank was the densely packed Old City, whose historic structures included the twelfth-century Grand al-Nouri Mosque—where the Islamic State's leader, Abu Bakr al-Baghdadi, had proclaimed the establishment of his caliphate in 2014. Characterized by narrow, winding alleyways and towering, multistory stone buildings, many with walled courtyards, the Old City provided an ideal stronghold for the Islamic State's defenders. Five bridges connected West Mosul to East Mosul, the latter of which encompassed an industrial district, the excavated ruins of the ancient Assyrian capital city of Nineveh, and the campus of the University of Mosul.[203]

Formerly the second-largest institution of higher education in Iraq, the university now served the Islamic State primarily as a barracks and weapons manufacturing plant. ISIS also took advantage of some of the university's laboratory facilities to produce rudimentary chemical weapons.[204]

As at Al Fallujah, the Islamic State had used its two-and-a-half-year occupation of Mosul to prepare a defensive network for the city. However, the Mosul fortifications were far more elaborate, reflecting the Islamic State's intention to hold the city at all costs. Underground tunnels ran throughout Mosul, connecting buildings, providing shelter from airstrikes, and concealing numerous supply and weapons caches. Obstacles, including disabled vehicles and concrete barriers, blocked roadways and channeled attackers into preselected "kill zones." Booby traps and IEDs of all kinds were ubiquitous, and ISIS rigged many buildings with explosives. Even the hundreds of thousands of civilians trapped in the city served a purpose, providing fighters with human shields. In Mosul, the Islamic State hoped, if possible, to defeat the Iraqi offensive outright. If this proved impossible, it intended to inflict such heavy casualties on the Iraqis that they would be unable to conduct subsequent operations.[205]

In view of the city's strong defenses, the ISF planned to approach the liberation of Mosul methodically (*Map 9*). The opening phase of the operation would involve an advance along two axes. While the Peshmerga cleared the approaches to East Mosul, proceeding from the northeast, PMF militia fighters would swing out to the west to cut ISIS's ground lines of communications. Meanwhile, coalition forces would carry out airstrikes to damage the bridges connecting East and West Mosul, partially isolating the ISIS forces east of the Tigris. The assault on the city proper—designated Operation EAGLE STRIKE—would then begin, with ISF units leapfrogging through the Peshmerga's lines and pushing into East Mosul. Once they secured the eastern part of the city, Iraqi forces would redeploy and execute the last stage of the offensive, the assault on West Mosul. Much like the liberation of Ar Ramadi the year before, the battle promised to be a months-long effort.[206] As President Obama stated on 18 October, "Mosul will be a difficult fight, and there will be advances and there will be setbacks. But I am confident that just as ISIL [ISIS] has been defeated in communities across Iraq, ISIL [ISIS] will be defeated in Mosul as well, and that will be another step towards their ultimate destruction."[207]

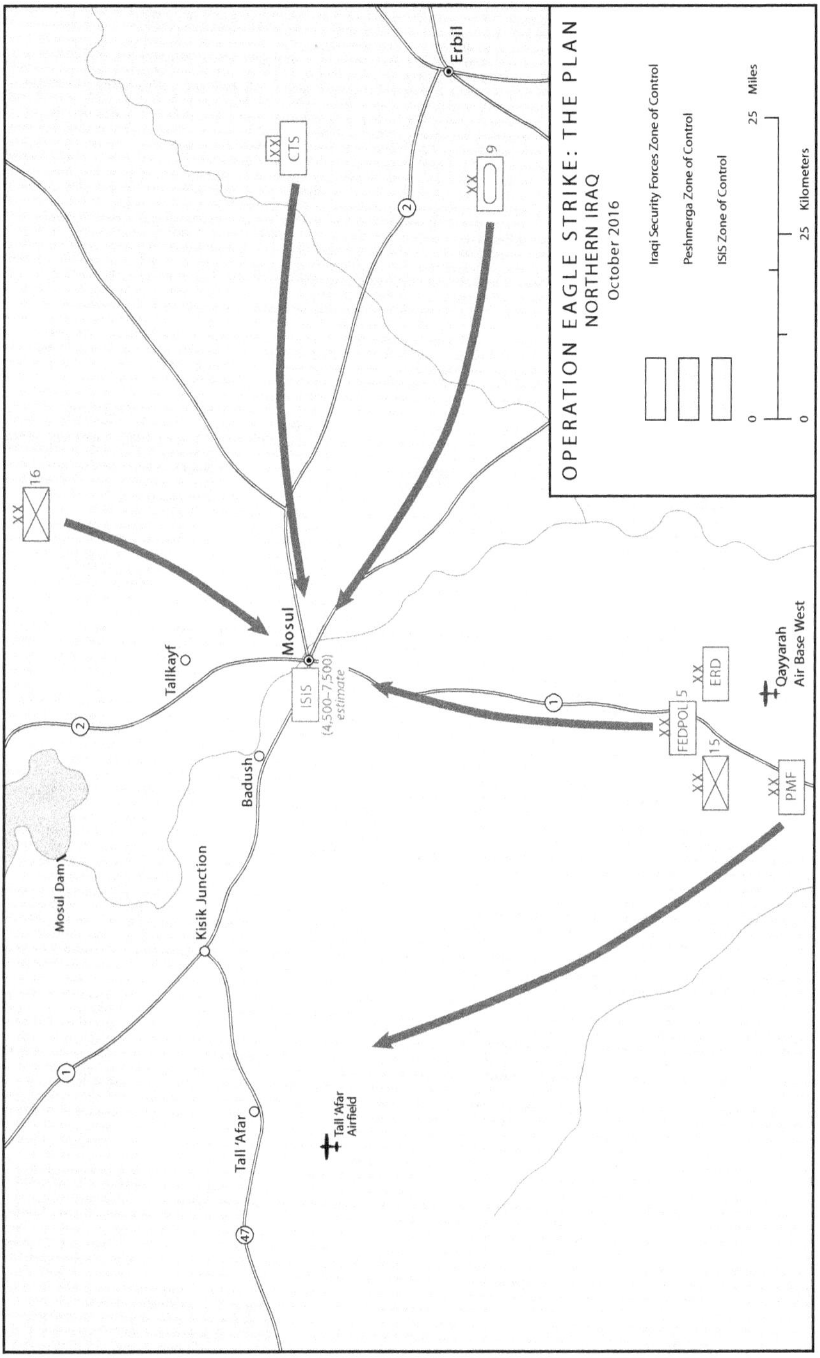

OPERATION EAGLE STRIKE: THE PLAN
NORTHERN IRAQ
October 2016

Iraqi Security Forces Zone of Control
Peshmerga Zone of Control
ISIS Zone of Control

0   25   Miles

0   25   Kilometers

Erbil

CTS

9

16

Mosul

ISIS
(4,500–7,500)
estimate

Tallkayf

Badush

Mosul Dam

Kisik Junction

FEDPOL 5

15

ERD

PMF

Qayyarah
Air Base West

Tall 'Afar
Airfield

Tall 'Afar

2

2

1

1

47

Map 9

Prime Minister al-Abadi announced the opening of the Mosul offensive on 16 October, and the Peshmerga began its advance toward East Mosul on the following day. Within a week, ISF units passed through the Kurdish lines, with the 16th Iraqi Army Division, Task Force CTS, and the 9th Iraqi Army Armored Division pushing toward the eastern half of Mosul on three separate axes. Two counterattacks by Islamic State forces surprised Task Force CTS but failed to halt its advance. By the end of the month, Iraqi forces were positioned to breach the outer perimeter of East Mosul (*Map 10*). Meanwhile, a simultaneous advance west of the Tigris, involving elements of the 5th Federal Police Division, the Emergency Response Division, and the 15th Iraqi Army Division, reached a point 15 kilometers south of the city. During the first two weeks of fighting, the ISF suffered about 300 casualties, including 130 soldiers killed in action. Of the Peshmerga's 200 casualties, 50 were killed in action.[208]

On 1 November, Iraqi forces entered the city limits of Mosul for the first time since June 2014, first reaching the eastern Al Karamah and Kukjali districts along the Erbil-Mosul highway.[209] ISIS quickly massed its forces to counter this threat, and resisted every fresh Iraqi advance, employing as many as sixty VBIEDs within the first month of combat. By mid-November, the 9th Iraqi Army Armored Division had halted, while Task Force CTS shifted its axis of advance toward the lightly defended neighborhoods to the northwest. The PMF units operating west of Mosul were more successful, capturing Tall 'Afar Air Base on 16 November with help from the 92d Brigade, 15th Iraqi Army Division, and tightening the ring around Mosul.[210] Despite this success, the end of November found the offensive stalled on all fronts, with only 30 percent of the city restored to Iraqi government control.[211]

Concerned about the lack of progress, General Townsend made several suggestions to the Iraqi high command for maintaining the offensive's momentum. Among these were that the ISF improve its management of logistics to ensure that frontline units received regular resupply, and that it implement countermeasures to limit the effectiveness of VBIEDs. Townsend also urged the ISF to use Iraqi Army and Federal Police units to hold liberated areas until local tribal and police units could be formed. For his part, he promised to deploy U.S. AH–64E Apache helicopters in direct support of Iraqi operations. On 1 December, General Townsend reported to CENTCOM that the

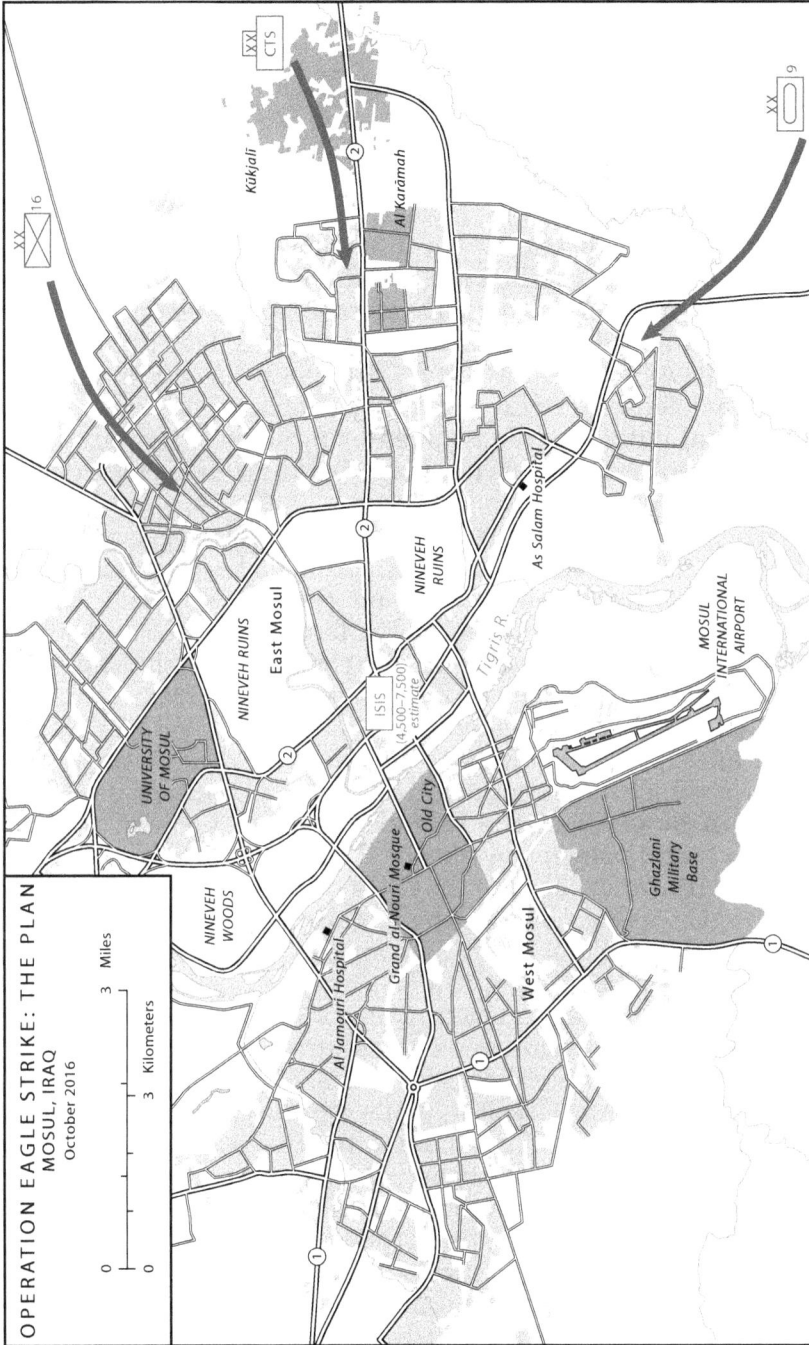

OPERATION EAGLE STRIKE: THE PLAN
MOSUL, IRAQ
October 2016

0   3   Miles
0   3   Kilometers

XX 16
XX CTS
XX 9

Kūkjalī
Al Karāmah

NINEVEH RUINS
East Mosul
NINEVEH RUINS
As Salam Hospital

Tigris R.

ISIS
(4,500–7,500
estimate)

UNIVERSITY
OF MOSUL

NINEVEH
WOODS

Old City
Grand al-Nouri Mosque

Al Jamouri Hospital

West Mosul

MOSUL
INTERNATIONAL
AIRPORT

Ghazlani
Military
Base

Map 10

Iraqi government had accepted his proposals and were in the process of implementing them.[212]

Shortly afterward, Iraqi forces attempted to regain the initiative with a surprise attack on As Salam Hospital, a suspected ISIS headquarters in southeast Mosul. At 0730 on 6 December, the 36th Brigade, 9th Iraqi Army Armored Division, began an advance toward the medical complex, located in a commercial district about 1.3 kilometers from the Tigris River. The brigade reached the facility and began to establish a defensive perimeter in the early afternoon. However, ISIS soon recovered and redeployed forces from East Mosul to meet this new threat. At 1800, a wave of SVBIEDs slammed into the 36th Brigade's defenses, forcing the Iraqi soldiers to shelter in one of the hospital buildings. Undeterred by airstrikes, militants took up positions in a nearby high-rise building and engaged the defenders with small-arms fire.

With the 36th Brigade effectively under siege, two CTS battalions redeployed overnight to spearhead a relief operation. Their attack kicked off at 1523 on the following day. Initial progress was swift, but heavy fire forced the CTS battalions to halt within 200 meters of the complex. Meanwhile, ISIS intensified its assault on the 36th Brigade. A barrage of rocket-propelled grenades, accompanied by another SVBIED attack, set off an explosive chain reaction that destroyed many of the brigade's vehicles and engulfed the hospital in flames. Unable to remain in position, the brigade's remnants joined up with the CTS battalions on the streets. The Iraqis then conducted a fighting withdrawal back to the ISF's front lines, reaching safety by 1838. Casualties during the engagement were heavy, with thirteen ISF soldiers killed and another forty-eight wounded. Additionally, thirteen Iraqi BMP–1 armored personnel carriers were destroyed or abandoned, along with five Humvees. ISIS suffered between seventy and one hundred casualties.[213]

The ISF immediately ceased offensive operations after the battle for As Salam Hospital, while significant reinforcements, including around 4,000 soldiers from the 5th Federal Police Division, flowed into southeast Mosul.[214] At the same time, General Townsend issued a tactical directive loosening the restrictions governing coalition ground operations. Published on 22 December, CJTF-OIR Tactical Directive 1 granted conventional coalition ground troops permission to accompany ISF units to the front lines—a privilege previously confined to special operations forces. The directive also granted coalition ground commanders greater discretion in selecting and approving targets for close air support and artillery fire.[215]

Responsibility for implementing these revised guidelines fell to a 500-person contingent from the 1st Infantry Division, which relieved General Volesky's 101st Airborne Division as CJFLCC-OIR headquarters on 17 November. Led by Maj. Gen. Joseph M. Martin, the 1st Infantry Division would direct coalition ground operations during the decisive phase of the battle for Mosul.[216] The 101st Airborne Division's 2d Brigade Combat Team likewise ended its deployment to Iraq in January 2017, handing over responsibility to Task Force FALCON, built around Col. J. Patrick Work's 2d Brigade Combat Team, 82d Airborne Division.[217]

The ISF returned to the offensive on 29 December, just one day after repulsing a major counterattack against the 16th Iraqi Army Division in northeast Mosul.[218] Attacking simultaneously along three axes, the Iraqis advanced at a rapid pace and surprised the Islamic State's overstretched defenders. On 8 January 2017, elements of Task Force CTS broke through to the Tigris River, cutting the caliphate's remaining territory in half.[219] With their perimeter quickly collapsing, the ISIS militants still east of the Tigris made their last stand on the campus of the University of Mosul. Using the university facilities as a defensive strongpoint, the militants resisted attacks by Task Force CTS and the 16th Iraqi Army Division for almost three days before withdrawing on 14 January.[220] On 24 January, Prime Minister al-Abadi announced that East Mosul was "fully liberated."[221]

This victory came only days after the inauguration of Donald J. Trump as president of the United States. For the most part, the new commander in chief followed the counter-ISIS strategy initiated under the Obama administration. The incoming secretary of defense, General (Ret.) James N. Mattis, embraced a more aggressive rhetoric, emphasizing the *annihilation* of the Islamic State (rather than *attrition*), but the liberation of Mosul proceeded more or less as planned.[222]

The Iraqi military took almost a month to prepare for the final phase of the offensive—the assault on West Mosul (*Map 11*). During this lull, an initial wave of 60,000 refugees returned to the city, as Mosul's civilian government resumed operations after two-and-a-half-years in exile. The 16th Iraqi Army Division also assumed authority as the "hold force" tasked with stabilizing East Mosul. Meanwhile, the other two major ISF formations east of the Tigris, the 9th Iraqi Army Armored Division and Task Force CTS, prepared to redeploy to the west. Once there, the 9th

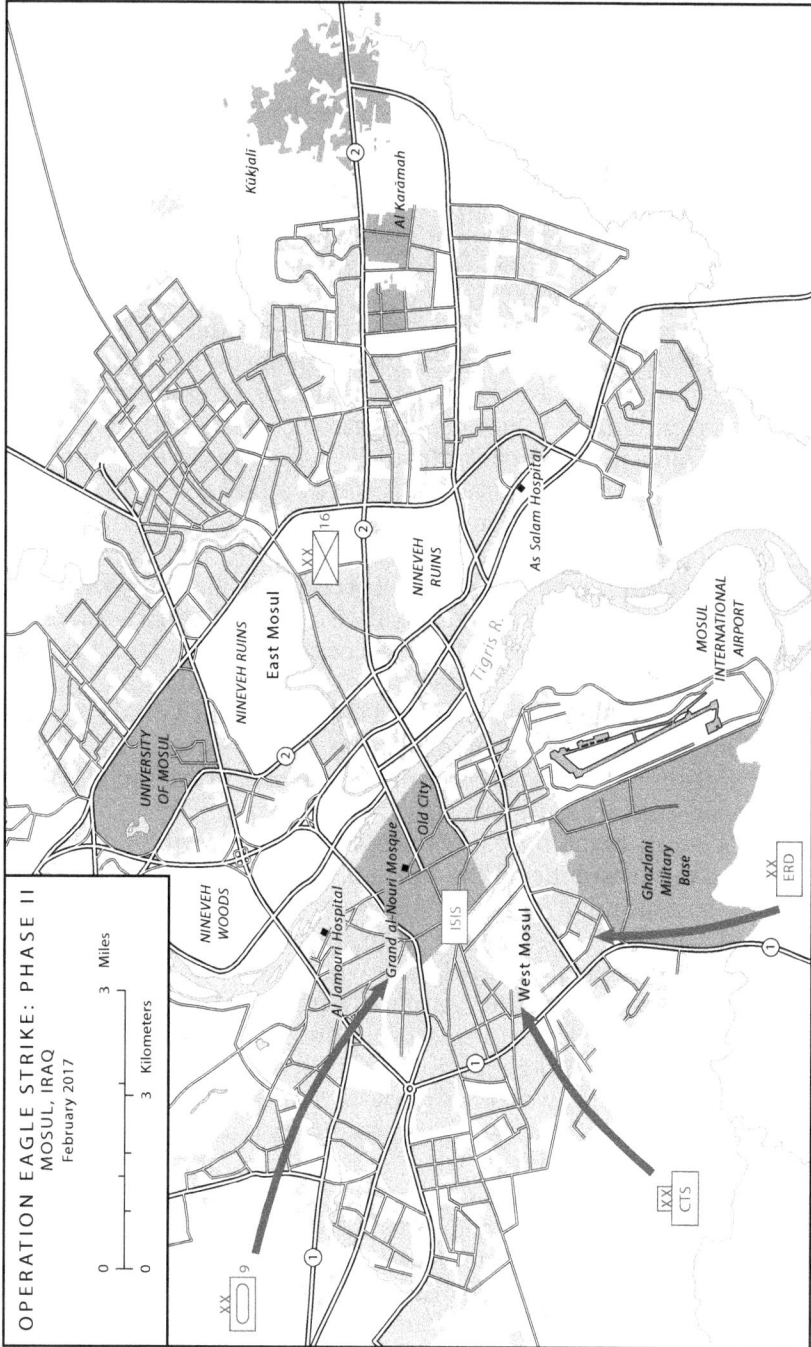

OPERATION EAGLE STRIKE: PHASE II
MOSUL, IRAQ
February 2017

Kūkjali

Al Karāmah

XX 16

NINEVEH RUINS

East Mosul

NINEVEH RUINS

As Salam Hospital

UNIVERSITY OF MOSUL

Tigris R.

MOSUL INTERNATIONAL AIRPORT

NINEVEH WOODS

Al Jamouri Hospital

Grand al-Nouri Mosque

Old City

ISIS

Ghazlani Military Base

West Mosul

XX ERD

XX 9

XX CTS

0   3   Miles
0   3   Kilometers

Map 11

Iraqi Army Armored Division would drive northwest through the open countryside west of Mosul, cutting Highway 1—the city's last significant ground line of communications—and seizing the town of Badush. The division would then join the assault on Mosul proper, advancing to the southeast. Following the same route, Task Force CTS would take up positions to attack along an east-west axis. Finally, the Emergency Response Division would continue its northward advance along the west bank of the Tigris. According to this plan, the ISIS garrison in West Mosul would face synchronized attacks on three fronts.[223]

The attack to clear West Mosul began on 19 February, with Federal Police units moving toward Mosul International Airport and the Ghazlani military base in the southwestern part of the city.[224] Both facilities fell to the Iraqi advance on 24 February.[225] The Islamic State continued to hold its positions stubbornly. In addition to VBIEDs, ISIS deployed swarms of store-bought quadcopter drones, which dropped 40-mm. grenades on Iraqi troops—a novel technique that the terrorist group had first introduced during the battle for East Mosul.[226] But while frequent conventional and unconventional counterattacks wore down the Iraqi forces, they did not stop the Iraqi advance. By the end of February, the Emergency Response Division was in possession of the southernmost of Mosul's five bridges, as well as adjacent neighborhoods on the west bank of the Tigris. Although heavily damaged by airstrikes, the bridge was still intact, and the Iraqis immediately began using it to transfer supplies across the river. Close by, Iraqi forces constructed a pontoon bridge connecting both banks of the Tigris. With this effort underway, the 9th Iraqi Army Armored Division completed the first stage of its flanking maneuver by cutting the Mosul–Tall 'Afar highway on 1 March. The division then drove on to Badush, capturing the riverfront town on 15 March.[227]

At the same time, the 16th Iraqi Army Division in East Mosul launched a limited operation aimed at clearing the countryside north of Mosul from Tallkayf to the Tigris River. Designated by the ISF as the "Sheik Muhammed Offensive," the operation took place with the advice and support of Task Force CHARGER, a U.S. Army contingent from the 1st Battalion, 12th Cavalry Regiment. The offensive made rapid progress and seized its objectives— although Iraqi forces failed to interdict the withdrawal of a large force of well-trained ISIS fighters, who escaped across the river to West Mosul, along with much of their equipment.[228]

Despite these setbacks, ISIS's resistance stiffened as the ISF pushed toward the terrorist group's fortified main line of resistance on the outskirts of West Mosul's Old City. Counterattacks, often featuring ISIS's vast arsenal of VBIEDs, took a heavy toll. In an attack on 15 March, ISIS militants loaded an armored construction vehicle with explosives and drove it through the Emergency Response Division's perimeter defenses. The ensuing explosion killed two soldiers and wounded twenty-two others. It also destroyed numerous vehicles, including an Iraqi T–72 tank and four Humvees. On another occasion, ISIS militants captured the commander of an Iraqi Federal Police battalion, together with his entire security detail—all of whom were later executed.[229] The ISF suffered nearly 3,500 casualties during the initial attacks on West Mosul, leading the Iraqis to suspend the offensive by the end of March.[230]

After pausing for more than a month to rest and refit, Iraqi forces resumed the offensive on 4 May, launching a major advance on Mosul from the northwest. The Emergency Response Division, which had relocated from its former area of operations south of Mosul, led the assault, supported on its right and left flanks by Task Force CTS and the 9th Iraqi Army Armored Division respectively. At the same time, Iraqi forces conducted subsidiary operations in the countryside to the west, with the PMF completing the encirclement of Tall 'Afar and arriving at the border near Mount Sinjar by the end of May.[231]

Fighting in Mosul during the following month centered on the outskirts of the Old City—the perimeter of the 5-square-kilometer pocket still under the terrorist group's control. Making use of the sewers and their own tunnel network, a company-sized force of ISIS fighters staged a last-ditch counterattack against the Federal Police units on the southern edge of the Old City on the morning of 14 June. The militants caught the Iraqis by surprise and killed around twenty policemen before the Iraqis managed to eliminate their assailants. The initiative then passed to the Iraqis, who devoted the remainder of the month to the capture of Al Jamouri Hospital—a modern medical complex, that served as an ISIS headquarters and fighting position north of the Old City. After several direct assaults on the hospital failed, Iraqi forces attempted to bypass it by pushing through to the Tigris River, reaching the waterway by 20 June. Iraqi forces then made another attempt to capture the facility by a direct assault on 25 June, although this failed as well. Following several airstrikes, which reduced much of the complex to rubble, the Emergency

The ruins of Grand al-Nouri Mosque, destroyed by ISIS fighters, in Mosul, Iraq, 14 May 2018. *(U.S. Army)*

Response Division made a final effort to clear the hospital on 30 June, securing it within forty-eight hours.[232]

With the hospital in Iraqi hands, the Islamic State held nothing except the battered ruins of the Old City itself. The last days of the battle for Mosul saw brutal street-by-street fighting in the district's congested alleyways. Anticipating defeat, ISIS militants blew up one of the city's most distinctive landmarks, the Grand al-Nouri Mosque, on 21 June. Elements of Task Force CTS reached the building's still-smoking ruins on 28 June.

With only a few pockets of ISIS holdouts remaining, Prime Minister al-Abadi publicly announced Mosul's liberation on 10 July. Hours after the prime minister's statement, however, around 200 militants strapped on suicide vests and approached Iraqi forces in an attempt to kill as many soldiers as possible. Fortunately, alert ISF troops spotted the attack—despite the militants' efforts to disguise themselves or feign surrender—and stopped most of the suicide bombers before they could reach Iraqi lines. The last ISIS strongpoint fell to Iraqi forces just under a week later, on 16 July, bringing the campaign to liberate Iraq's third-largest city to a close. The final stage of the battle was particularly bloody, as ISIS militants fought desperately with

59

little thought for personal preservation. The ISF suffered around 3,710 casualties between 4 May and 16 July, including 610 soldiers killed in action. Iraqi losses during the entire nine-month battle amounted to 1,320 soldiers killed and 6,880 wounded.[233]

Two members of CJTF-OIR also were killed in action during Operation EAGLE STRIKE. CPO Jason C. Finan fell to an IED while serving with the U.S. Navy's Explosive Ordnance Disposal Mobile Unit Three at Ba'shiqah, 16 kilometers north of Mosul, on 20 October 2016.[234] On 29 April 2017, 1st Lt. Weston C. Lee died as a result of an IED explosion while advising Kurdish forces near Mosul. He had deployed to Iraq as part of the 1st Battalion, 325th Infantry Regiment.[235]

These losses underscored the extent of the coalition's support for the Iraqi offensive. In accordance with Tactical Directive 1, Task Force FALCON formed mobile advisory teams, equipped with their own security details and armored vehicles, and worked directly with Iraqi brigade headquarters in the field. Some coalition advisers partnered with ISF units down to the platoon level.[236] During the battle for Mosul's Old City in June and July, when the close proximity of the two sides limited the effectiveness of airstrikes, CJTF-OIR personnel even engaged in combat with ISIS forces directly, using standoff weapons like sniper rifles and antitank guided missiles.[237]

Air support also played a crucial role in the Iraqi victory. Coalition ground force commanders made extensive use of the authority delegated to them by General Townsend, calling in numerous airstrikes on ISIS positions in support of their Iraqi partners. Of the 16,574 strikes carried out around Mosul between 17 October 2016 and 12 July 2017, approximately 90 percent were against targets of opportunity, requested by coalition or Iraqi officers in response to developing conditions on the battlefield, rather than preplanned missions.[238] The coalition's high degree of responsiveness to requests for fire support emboldened Iraqi commanders to maneuver against the enemy much more aggressively. Indeed, coalition advisers found that the Iraqis benefited from "motivational fires"—indirect fire targeting "non-essential or benign targets" along the path of a planned ISF movement.[239]

In this way, as in others, coalition forces adapted themselves to their host-nation partners, providing "assurance" as well as advice. As General Martin noted, "The philosophy was to quit trying to make them (Iraqis) us, they are not us. They are never going to be us. Their tactics are never going to be ours. They are Iraqis."[240] That realization represented an important breakthrough. Rather than trying to "fix" the Iraqis by turning the ISF into a Middle Eastern version of the U.S. military, advisers altered their approaches to best suit the conditions at hand, regardless of the problems or frustrations they encountered along the way. The result was a major strategic victory over the Islamic State.

OPERATION ECLIPSE: THE LIBERATION OF AR RAQQAH, 2016–2017

While the ISF fought through the streets of Mosul, a parallel campaign played out in the heart of the Islamic State's caliphate, the Syrian city of Ar Raqqah. Captured by ISIS in early 2014, Ar Raqqah had languished under the terrorist group's rule for the better part of three years. Liberating it would not be an easy task. The city lay deep within the Islamic State's Syrian territory along the banks of the Euphrates. To reach it, the coalition's proxies—the SDF—would have to cross at least 50 kilometers of desert and overcome between 900 and 1,600 ISIS militants occupying various positions in the surrounding countryside. Once they reached Ar Raqqah, the SDF would then have to fight through a congested urban environment against a determined and well-prepared opponent. The 2,000 ISIS militants defending the city had stockpiles of small arms, IEDs, and chemical weapons.[241] Ar Raqqah's ancient multistory stone buildings and modern high-rises—buttressed by obstacle belts, earthen berms, and trenches—served as ideal fighting positions.[242] Finally, the central Old City, with its 11-meter-tall mud-brick walls, was a veritable fortress in its own right—nearly as formidable in the twenty-first century as it had been when it was originally constructed almost fourteen hundred years before.[243]

To capture this objective, the SDF could call on some 45,000 fighters. Around 13,000 were members of the Syrian Arab Coalition. The remaining 32,000 fighters belonged mainly to the Kurdish YPG.[244] By the end of 2016, only fighters affiliated with various Syrian Arab Coalition groups—fewer than 3,000 in total—had received training and equipment from the coalition.[245] Neither faction possessed much heavy military equipment. The rank-and-file wielded small arms, rocket launchers, and simple crew-served weapons. Few had access to basic protective gear, like helmets and body armor. For mobility, they relied primarily on civilian vehicles, including pickup trucks with heavy machine guns mounted behind the cab. Nevertheless, the SDF was highly effective on the battlefield. Hardened by years of warfare, it employed a tactical approach characterized

61

Female SDF trainees, both Arab and Kurdish volunteers, stand in formation at their graduation ceremony in northern Syria, 9 August 2017. *(U.S. Army)*

by speed, stealth, and surprise. This formula proved consistently successful against the Islamic State.[246]

Within CJTF-OIR, responsibility for overseeing the liberation of Ar Raqqah fell to Special Operations Joint Task Force–Operation INHERENT RESOLVE (SOJTF-OIR), a division-level headquarters under the tactical control of General Townsend. Commanded by Maj. Gen. James E. Kraft Jr., SOJTF-OIR fielded around 2,000 U.S. troops in Syria by the end of 2017. These forces assisted their partners in various ways as trainers, combat advisers, and forward air controllers. They also provided the SDF with access to cutting-edge communications technology that enhanced the militia's ability to operate on the battlefield.[247]

The coalition conceived of the campaign to liberate Ar Raqqah—designated Operation ECLIPSE—as a methodical, multiphase offensive. The SDF would secure several intermediate objectives before encircling Ar Raqqah itself. It would then attack the city from the north, east, and west.[248] Coalition air support would play a crucial role throughout the operation, compensating for the militia's lack of heavy weapons and equipment (*Map 12*).[249]

The offensive began on 5 November 2016.[250] During the first month, the SDF advanced southward steadily toward Ar Raqqah, meeting only light resistance. By the end of the year, the SDF had covered roughly half the distance to the city, clearing almost 1,300 square kilometers and freeing thousands of civilians from ISIS's rule.[251] Progress along the western axis of advance was especially significant. By 12 January 2017, the SDF had liberated almost the entire eastern shore of Lake Assad, approaching within 5 kilometers of the Tabqa Dam.[252] Recapturing the dam itself was an immediate operational priority, as media reports suggested that it was close to collapse. This precarious situation added impetus to the coalition's plans to secure the site before advancing on Ar Raqqah. The nearby town of Al Tabaqah (Ath Thawrah), a local ISIS headquarters and logistics hub, was also an important intermediate objective.[253]

To provide further support, the Pentagon deployed an additional 400 military personnel to Syria in March. This deployment included an artillery detachment from the 11th Marine Expeditionary Unit, which would provide indirect fire support for the SDF, and elements from the 75th Ranger Regiment, which would help deter a threatened Turkish attack on Manbij.[254] The latter move was in response to escalating Turkish-Kurdish tensions, which posed a significant threat to the campaign. Between August 2016 and February 2017, Turkish-backed Syrian rebels captured the Syrian cities of Jarabulus and Al Bab, with support from the Turkish armed forces. Although the Turkish government insisted that their operations were directed against the Islamic State, Turkish forces clashed with the SDF on several occasions. The assault on Al Bab, in particular, thwarted the PYD's long-cherished objective of connecting the isolated Kurdish canton of 'Afrin in western Syria with the autonomous Kurdish cantons to the east. Fearing an imminent Turkish attack on Manbij, just east of Al Bab, the SDF prepared to redeploy its forces from the Ar Raqqah offensive to defend its territory. The arrival of U.S. troops in Manbij mitigated these concerns, making it possible for the SDF to continue its offensive without fearing an attack on its western flank.[255]

While the SDF and its accompanying coalition advisers prepared for the assault on Al Tabaqah, the militia's forces

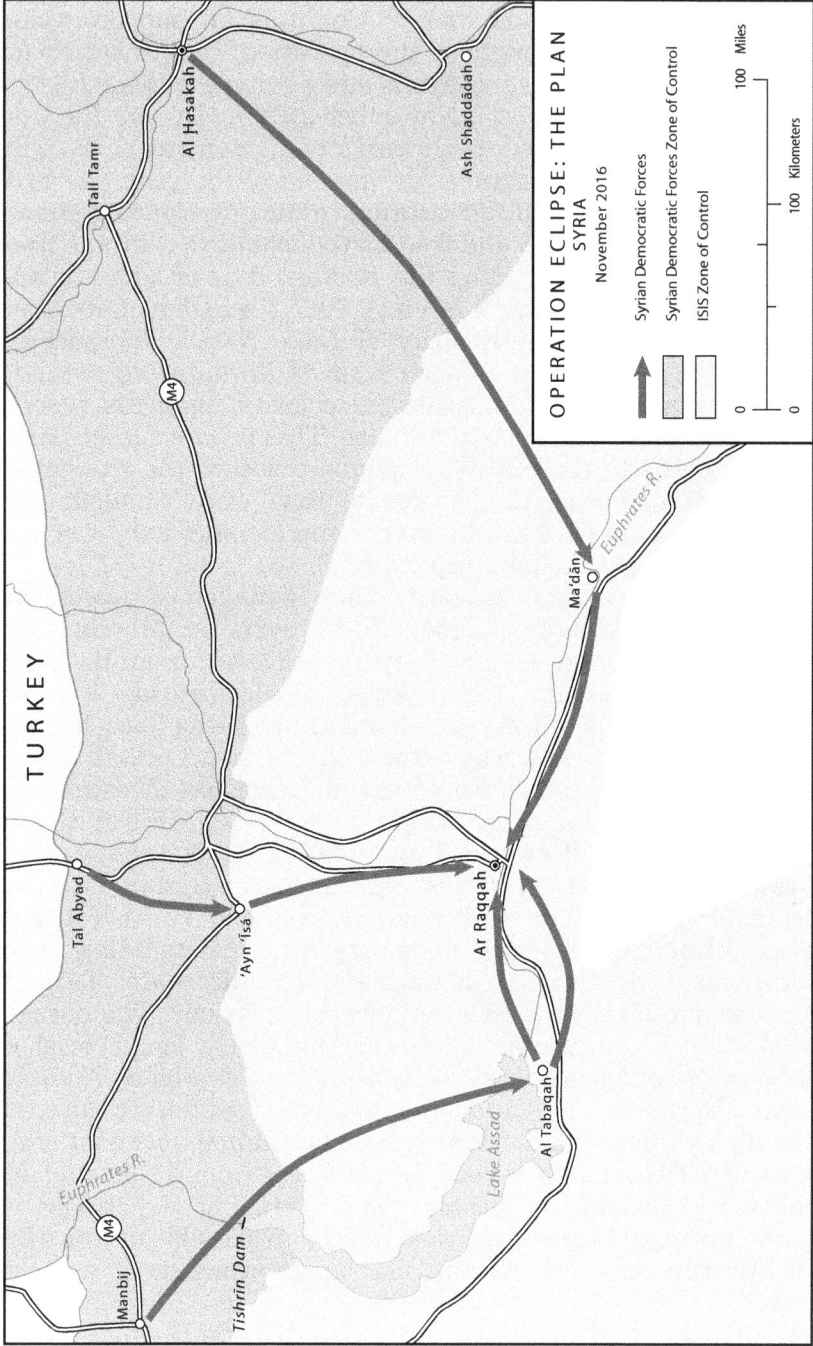

OPERATION ECLIPSE: THE PLAN
SYRIA
November 2016

Syrian Democratic Forces
Syrian Democratic Forces Zone of Control
ISIS Zone of Control

Miles
0   100
Kilometers
0   100

TURKEY

Al Hasakah
Tall Tamr
Ash Shaddādah
M4
Ma'dān
Euphrates R.
Tal Abyad
'Ayn 'Īsā
Ar Raqqah
Al Tabaqah
Lake Assad
Euphrates R.
M4
Manbij
Tishrin Dam

Map 12

swept through the countryside north and east of Ar Raqqah. Between 4 and 24 February, the Islamic State lost control of nearly one hundred villages as the SDF elements closed to within 5 kilometers of Ar Raqqah. At the same time, the SDF cut the Ar Raqqah–Hasakah highway, isolating the terrorist group's capital from its territory in Syria's southeastern Dayr as Zawr Province.[256]

Finally, following weeks of planning and rehearsals, the SDF launched their attack on Al Tabaqah on the evening of 21 March. The coalition played a key role in the operation, with U.S. helicopters and Osprey tilt rotor aircraft transporting around 400 SDF fighters across Lake Assad in a daring air assault. Accompanied by coalition advisers, the militia forces advanced on the city from the south, catching the Islamic State's garrison in Al Tabaqah by surprise and cutting the Aleppo–Ar Raqqah highway. Other SDF fighters crossed Lake Assad on barges, bringing reinforcements, supplies, and equipment. Over the following days, the Islamic State's forces regrouped and fought back with determination, leading to a protracted and bloody engagement that continued throughout the month of April. By the beginning of May, however, ISIS's position in Al Tabaqah was no longer tenable. Rather than fighting to the death, the Islamist group negotiated a truce with the SDF and abandoned the city, leaving behind their heavy weapons and disabling their remaining IEDs. In accordance with this arrangement, ISIS forces formed a convoy and departed Al Tabaqah on 10 May. Although the negotiated settlement surprised the coalition, CJTF-OIR seized the opportunity to carry out several airstrikes on the convoy, destroying some equipment before it dispersed.[257]

The victory at Al Tabaqah set the conditions for the SDF's final advance on Ar Raqqah. In preparation for this attack, the United States expanded its support for the SDF to include the YPG as well as the Syrian Arab Coalition, despite the Turkish government's objections.[258] The first shipment of small arms, mortars, and armored vehicles reached the SDF in late May.[259] The initial assault on the Islamic State's capital began only a few days later—just as Iraqi forces were closing in on the last pocket of ISIS resistance in West Mosul. Supported by coalition airstrikes and artillery fire, SDF elements pushed into Ar Raqqah on 5 June (*Map 13*). The SDF moved rapidly through the Al Mishlab neighborhood in eastern Ar Raqqah, reaching the ancient city walls.[260] Progress on the western axis was almost as swift, as the coalition-backed fighters occupied the ruins of

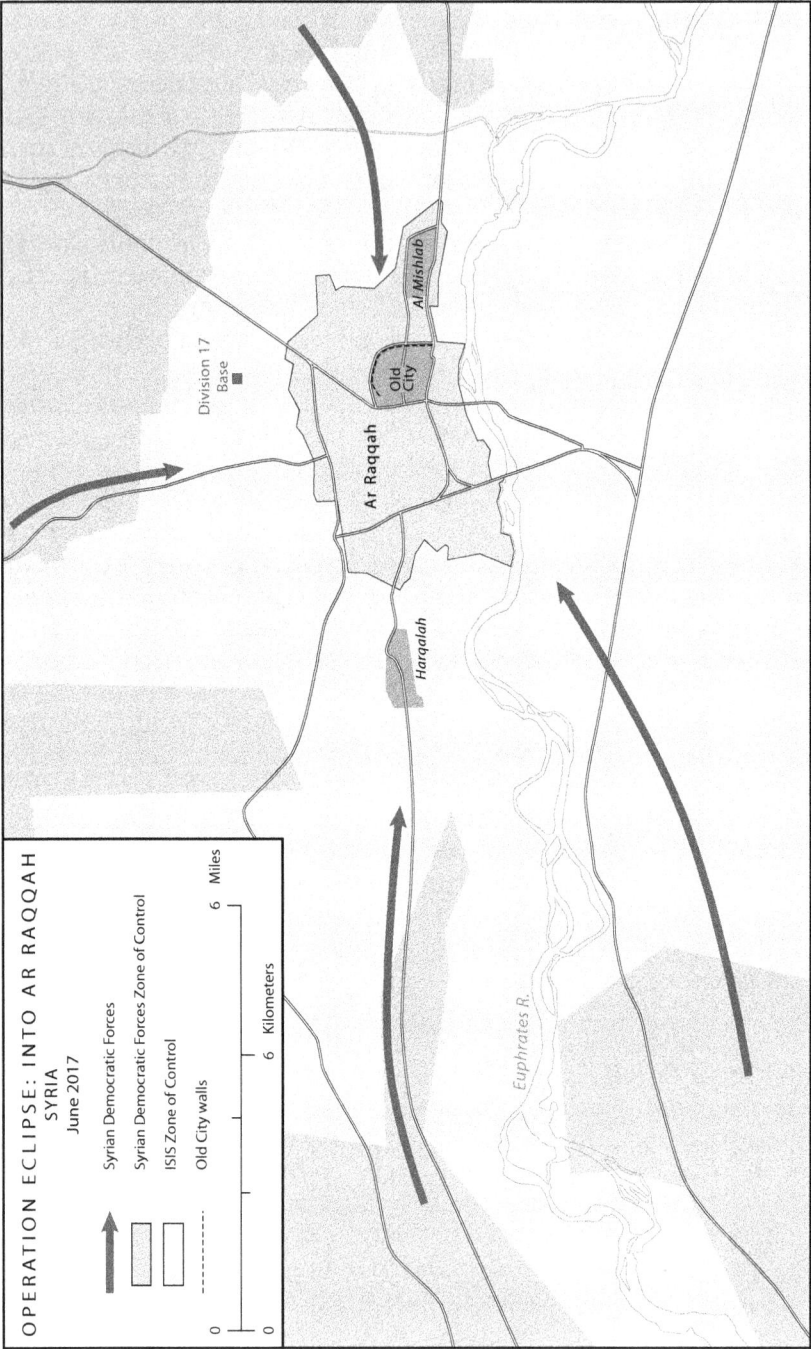

OPERATION ECLIPSE: INTO AR RAQQAH
SYRIA
June 2017

Syrian Democratic Forces
Syrian Democratic Forces Zone of Control
ISIS Zone of Control
Old City walls

0   6   Kilometers
0   6   Miles

Division 17
Base

Ar Raqqah

Al Mishlab

Old City

Harqalah

Euphrates R.

Map 13

the medieval Harqalah fortress.[261] Meanwhile, a simultaneous advance along the southern bank of the Euphrates completed the isolation of the city, cutting off its last connection with the caliphate's territory to the southeast.[262] Within two weeks, the SDF had pushed the Islamic State's forces back to the Old City.

Although fierce, ISIS's resistance in Ar Raqqah was noticeably weaker than it had been during the opening phase of the battle for Mosul. Many ISIS militants had roots in Iraq, but the Islamic State's connection with its so-called capital was more recent and arguably more superficial. Locals obeyed ISIS out of fear and opportunism, rather than loyalty. They consequently showed less determination to defend the city against the coalition than the die-hards in Mosul. Their tepid support left a smaller core of foreign fighters to carry the burden of defending Ar Raqqah—and even these were less motivated than their counterparts in Iraq, as most of the Islamic State's senior leaders had evacuated the area months before the SDF reached the city limits.[263]

By the end of June, however, the Islamic State's defenders in the Old City, taking maximum advantage of Ar Raqqah's defensive walls, threatened to halt the SDF's offensive. Breaks in the ancient fortifications channeled attacking troops into minefields and through kill zones overlooked by prepared fighting positions, and the SDF was unable to push into the Old City without taking excessive casualties. To clear a path, on 3 July coalition aircraft carried out targeted strikes on two 25-meter sections of the city walls. SDF elements immediately poured through the breaches, bypassing ISIS's defenses and securing a lodgment 300 meters inside the outer walls.[264]

This marked the beginning of a new phase of the battle. During the following weeks, the coalition-backed militia fought street by street through Ar Raqqah's Old City against stiffening ISIS resistance. On 14 August, ISIS forces attempted a general counterattack, using multiple SVBIEDs to break the SDF's lines. This response caused momentary confusion, but the SDF quickly regrouped and repulsed the assault with support from coalition airstrikes and artillery fire. ISIS suffered around 220 casualties before withdrawing.[265]

Afterward, the Islamic State remained on the defensive, falling back in the face of the SDF's determined advance. Although the SDF announced the liberation of Ar Raqqah on 1 September, fighting continued for weeks after, with the last ISIS stronghold in the northern part of the city falling to the SDF on 14 September. In this phase, the Islamic State's most effective weapons were IEDs, which it used extensively to impede the SDF's advance. Individual city blocks could contain as many as several thousand of the devices.[266] But even though such obstacles enabled ISIS to hold out much longer than otherwise would have been possible, they could not turn the tide of battle. In late September and early October, the remaining ISIS holdouts made a last stand in the center of the city. They accepted the SDF's offer of a conditional surrender on 15 October. As at Al Tabaqah, the SDF permitted the surviving ISIS militants to collect their families and evacuate the city with their weapons. The SDF took control on 17 October.[267]

The price of victory was high. The SDF lost more than 650 fighters during the battle.[268] Two coalition service members also were killed in action. On 24 November 2016, SCPO Scott C. Dayton, of the U.S. Navy's Explosive Ordnance Disposal Mobile Unit Two, died when an IED exploded in Ayn Isa.[269] On 23 September 2017, Adjudant-Chef Stéphane Grenier, a special operations soldier in France's 13th Parachute Dragoon Regiment, fell in an operation on the Syrian-Iraqi border.[270] Finally, Ar Raqqah's inhabitants suffered worst of all. Around 1,000 civilians were killed in the battle, while a further 270,000 residents were displaced.[271] Months of airstrikes and street fighting left the city utterly desolated. In the words of one eyewitness, "Every building seemed to have been struck by ordnance: either destroyed entirely, scorched black by fire, or in a state of mid-collapse. . . . Smoke and dust roiled over rooftops."[272] Reconstruction promised to be a mammoth endeavor.

The future of Ar Raqqah—like that of Syria as a whole—was ambiguous. After crushing the strongest opposition groups in western Syria in 2016, Bashar al-Assad's brutal Russian- and Iranian-backed government shifted its forces eastward. During the first half of 2017, the regime captured several ISIS strongholds, including Palmyra, and encroached on territory held by the coalition's partners. On 17 May, a convoy of pro–Assad regime military units entered the wide exclusion zone that CJTF-OIR had established around the Vetted Syrian Opposition training outpost at At Tanf in southeastern Syria. When these forces refused to withdraw after repeated warnings, coalition aircraft struck the convoy with precision guided munitions on 18 May, destroying two vehicles. A second incursion on 5 June met with a similarly kinetic response. Two further clashes with progovernment forces took place before the end of June, as both sides refused to back down. Meanwhile, Syrian regime forces operating to the north reached the banks of the Euphrates River, where they skirmished with SDF elements on the opposite shore. To head off a wider conflict, General Townsend and his Russian counterpart agreed to separate the SDF from the Syrian regime and its armed supporters with a line of demarcation that ran along the Euphrates from Al Tabaqah to Ar Raqqah.[273]

The XVIII Airborne Corps departed the theater of operations on 5 September, handing over authority to the III Corps, commanded by now Lt. Gen. Paul E. Funk II.[274] CJFLCC-OIR also changed hands during the summer, transitioning from the 1st Infantry Division, under General Martin, to the 1st Armored Division, headed by Maj. Gen. Robert P. White.[275] With the Islamic State's forces in disarray, Operation INHERENT RESOLVE entered its third phase on 8 August.[276] This important step was a fitting conclusion to both tours. At Mosul, the ISF had prevailed in a grueling urban battle. The battle for Ar Raqqah, while on a smaller scale, had been an equally impressive triumph for the militia fighters of the SDF.

THE END OF THE CALIPHATE, 2017–2020

The strategic situation that confronted General Funk in September 2017 differed greatly from what he had found on his first deployment in support of Operation INHERENT RESOLVE. During the three years since the initial American intervention, the U.S.-led coalition had reduced the Islamic State from a seemingly unstoppable force to a battered husk with only a fraction of its former territory and resources. But for General Funk, the most salient difference was the vast improvement in the ISF. As he noted, initially the Iraqis were "running away, abandoning their equipment; basically the army could not conduct any effective offensive or defensive operations. But three years later they are executing a division level attack [near the Syrian border]."[277]

During the first part of the III Corps' rotation, Iraqi forces put these hard-won skills to good use as they eliminated the last remaining ISIS enclaves on Iraqi soil. This process began before General Funk's arrival, shortly after the fall of Mosul. On 20 August, the ISF launched an assault on Tall 'Afar. Within a week, the city was in Iraqi hands.[278] In September, the Iraqi military pivoted east to clear a pocket of ISIS territory around the city of Al Hawijah. In a sign that the Islamic State's morale was crumbling—at least in Iraq—hundreds of ISIS fighters surrendered instead of fighting to the death. Iraqi forces secured the city on 5 October.[279] The Iraqis then resumed the offensive in western Al Anbar Province, capturing the border crossing of Al Qa'im on 3 November. Rawah, the last ISIS-held town in Iraq, fell to the ISF on 17 November.[280] Less than a month later, Prime Minister al-Abadi formally declared victory over the Islamic State.[281]

The final victories in Iraq did not come without a cost. The ISF suffered almost 800 casualties, including 115 soldiers killed in action, during the battle for Tall 'Afar alone.[282] Coalition forces also suffered losses. Seven members of CJTF-OIR were injured—two fatally—when a 155-mm. artillery round prematurely exploded on 13 August 2017, mortally wounding Sgt. Roshain E. Brooks and Sgt. Allen L. Stigler. Their unit, Battery C, 2d Battalion (Airborne), 319th Field Artillery Regiment, had been firing on an ISIS mortar position near Tall 'Afar.[283] Another death came on 1 October, when an IED struck a coalition convoy near Q-West Airfield, killing Spc. Alexander W. Missildine. A second soldier, Sfc. David Mathis, suffered serious injuries in the same blast, losing both of his legs.[284]

In early 2018, CJTF-OIR scaled back its tactical and operational support to the ISF. Rather than continuing to advise Iraqi formations on the battlefield, the command tailored its training and advisory mission to assist with the ISF's efforts to hold newly liberated territory and to prevent the rise of an ISIS insurgency.[285] Above all, the coalition sought to ensure that the Iraqi military could sustain the level of competence it had demonstrated during the battles for Mosul and Tall 'Afar.

The new phase of the campaign in Iraq, designated Operation RELIABLE PARTNERSHIP, saw a diminished need for coalition ground troops.[286] General Funk accordingly inactivated CJFLCC-OIR at the end of April—less than two months after the 1st Armored Division had transferred authority for the land component command to the 10th Mountain Division under Maj. Gen. Walter E. Piatt. This decision marked the end of the headquarters that had exercised continuous control over conventional coalition ground operations in Iraq for almost four years.[287]

It was evident by the end of General Funk's tour in September 2018 that ISIS no longer posed an existential threat to the Iraqi government. The group's territorial control in Iraq was minimal. Its fighters were reduced to operating entirely as insurgents, usually under cover of darkness. Rather than conquering cities and governing hundreds of thousands, they planted roadside bombs and assassinated village elders. These activities were

Maj. Gen. Walter Piatt, commander of Combined Joint Forces Land Component Command (CJFLCC), shakes hands with Iraqi staff Lt. Gen. Abdul Amir al-Lami, deputy commander of Iraq Joint Operations Command, during the CJFLCC deactivation ceremony in Baghdad, 30 April 2018. *(U.S. Army)*

abhorrent, and required constant vigilance from the ISF, but they had only a limited strategic impact.[288] Despite ISIS's best efforts, Iraqi civilian casualties attributable to terrorism fell to record lows during 2018.[289] Moreover, the Iraqi parliamentary elections in May—the first since the fall of Mosul in 2014—went relatively smoothly.[290] After four years of war, Iraq seemed to be returning to some form of normalcy.

Perhaps the main threat to Iraq's stability at this juncture was the fraught relationship between the KRG and the Iraqi national government in Baghdad. In September 2017, disputes over territory that the Peshmerga had occupied since 2014 nearly led to open warfare between the two groups. Acting unilaterally, the KRG held an independence referendum on 25 September, tallying votes throughout the entire region under Kurdish control—including areas, like Kirkuk, that legally fell under the jurisdiction of the Iraqi central government.[291] One month later, the Iraqi government responded with a brief and relatively bloodless military campaign that resulted in the recapture of all of the disputed territories by the beginning of November. Conflict between the Peshmerga and the ISF was a boon for the

Islamic State. In the following months, ISIS took advantage of the breakdown in cooperation between the two security forces to carry out a renewed insurgent campaign along the "green line" separating the KRG from the rest of Iraq. Kirkuk, in particular, became a center of ISIS activity.[292]

The ongoing violence in Iraq, although concerning, paled in comparison to the turmoil in Syria. In early September 2017, Syrian regime forces reached the city of Dayr as Zawr, which had been held in part by the Islamic State for three years. They secured the city, most of which lay on the south bank of the Euphrates, by early November.[293] Syrian government forces then swept to the southeast, occupying nearly the entire 115-kilometer stretch of the Euphrates between the city of Dayr as Zawr and the Iraqi border by the end of the year. Supported by CJTF-OIR, the SDF rushed to occupy the opposite shore, as well as the triangle of largely uninhabited desert between the Euphrates and the Iraqi border. By January 2018, the Islamic State found its caliphate reduced to a few villages in Syria's Middle Euphrates River Valley (*Map 14*).[294]

The Islamic State's rapid collapse brought the SDF and the Syrian regime into contact along a wide front. For months, the two sides maintained an uneasy truce, punctuated by occasional skirmishes. On 7 February, however, this state of semipeaceful coexistence ended abruptly when a battalion-sized force of proregime mercenaries launched a surprise assault on an SDF headquarters near the Conoco gas field outside the city of Dayr as Zawr. Supported by twenty-seven vehicles, including several armored personnel carriers and at least three T–72 tanks, the detachment slowly maneuvered into position before opening fire and bombarding the U.S.-backed forces with artillery and tank rounds. The barrage pinned down the defenders, including around thirty U.S. special operations troops who were visiting the outpost. After several fruitless attempts to contact the assailants—and after receiving confirmation from the Russian headquarters in Syria that the mercenaries were not operating under their command—U.S. forces responded in kind, carrying out airstrikes using drones, stealth fighters, and attack helicopters. Meanwhile, a sixteen-person coalition quick reaction force rushed to assist from a nearby base. The proregime detachment withdrew early in the morning on 8 February, leaving behind between 200 and 300 fighters killed in action. None of the U.S. soldiers was injured.[295]

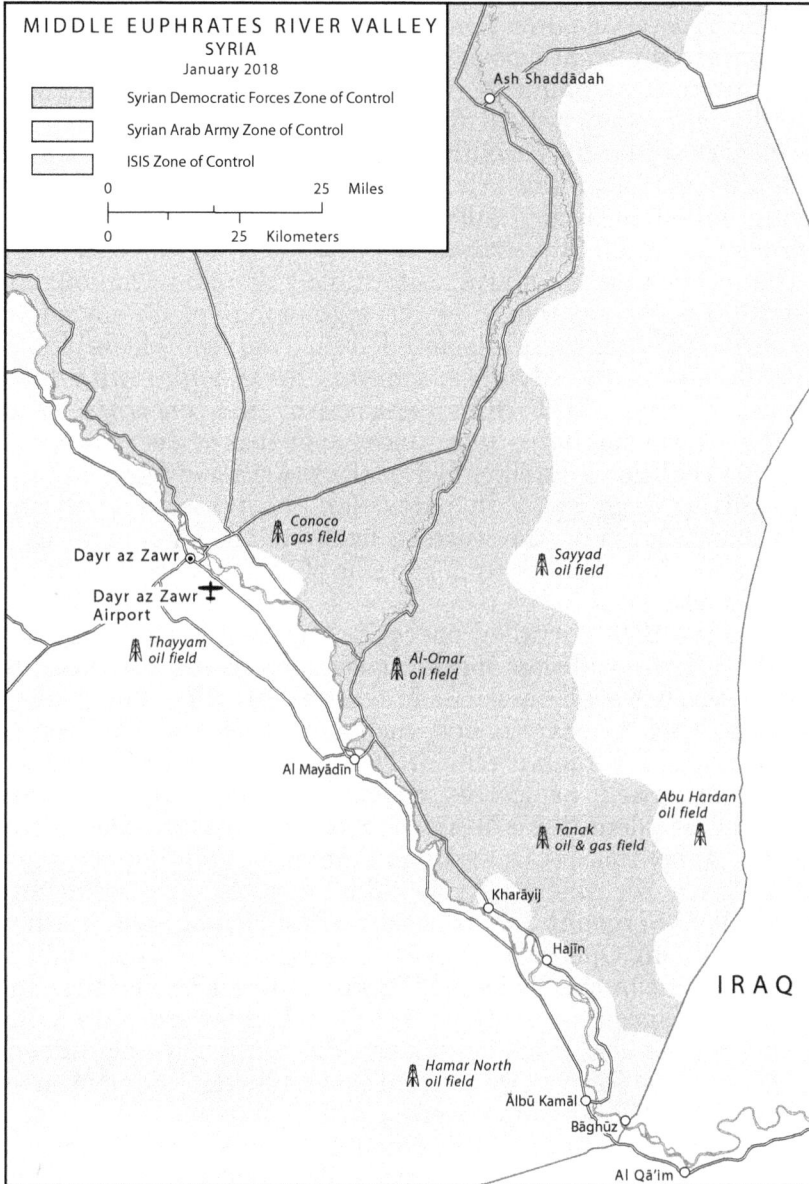

MIDDLE EUPHRATES RIVER VALLEY
SYRIA
January 2018

Syrian Democratic Forces Zone of Control

Syrian Arab Army Zone of Control

ISIS Zone of Control

Map 14

The mercenaries' attack came only weeks after the Turkish armed forces launched an offensive against the YPG-controlled 'Afrin District in northwestern Syria.[296] Open conflict between the coalition's Syrian proxy and Turkey, a NATO (North

73

Atlantic Treaty Organization) ally, placed the United States in an awkward diplomatic position. It also threatened to derail the SDF's ground campaign against ISIS, as hundreds of Kurdish SDF fighters redeployed to 'Afrin from Ar Raqqah and Dayr as Zawr.[297] Despite these reinforcements, Turkish-backed forces took full control of the 'Afrin District by the end of March, having killed around 1,500 Kurdish fighters and displaced approximately 200,000 civilians.[298]

The incident at 'Afrin provided a timely respite to the Islamic State.[299] Taking advantage of the operational pause forced on the SDF, ISIS militants displaced from Iraq and elsewhere in Syria flocked to the Middle Euphrates River Valley with their families.[300] From CJTF-OIR's perspective, this concentration of ISIS forces was not entirely unwelcome, as it provided a tangible target for coalition airstrikes.[301] But the situation in Dayr as Zawr was still far from ideal. In particular, the presence of Syrian government forces on the western banks of the Euphrates gave ISIS the freedom to move from one side of the river to the other to evade attacks.

While the SDF curtailed operations against ISIS during the fight for 'Afrin, coalition special operations forces continued to conduct smaller-scale missions in conjunction with their Syrian partners. In late March, one such operation—an attempt to kill or capture a high-profile ISIS member in Manbij—ended in tragedy when explosives carried by the coalition team detonated accidentally, killing M. Sgt. Jonathan J. Dunbar of the U.S. Army Special Operations Command and Sgt. Matthew Tonroe from the British Army's 3d Battalion, the Parachute Regiment.[302] Sergeant Tonroe was the first British soldier killed in action during Operation INHERENT RESOLVE. Five other soldiers were wounded in the incident.[303] Similar direct-action missions by coalition special operations forces took a severe toll on the Islamic State's senior leadership but did not receive significant media coverage—except in unusual cases, like the raid in Manbij, where CJTF-OIR personnel were killed.[304]

The SDF's assault on ISIS's redoubt in the Middle Euphrates River Valley, designated Operation ROUNDUP, began in May. During the first stage of the offensive, the SDF consolidated control over the Syrian-Iraqi border and encircled ISIS's remaining territory along the Euphrates River. Within two weeks, the militia controlled the border town of Baghuz.[305] The SDF then pushed eastward from the town of Ash Shaddadah before turning south and sweeping across the desert to the

General Funk (second from right) meets with SDF commander General Mazloum. *(Combined Joint Task Force-Operation INHERENT RESOLVE)*

Euphrates.[306] The coalition provided extensive air support to the SDF throughout these operations, executing more than 500 strikes between 1 May and 3 August.[307]

The final phase of Operation ROUNDUP—the attack on the last pocket of territory near the village of Hajin—began on 10 September 2018.[308] Three days later, General Funk transferred authority back to the XVIII Airborne Corps, now commanded by Lt. Gen. Paul J. LaCamera. Under Funk, CJTF-OIR had sustained the momentum generated by the Iraqi victory at the battle for Mosul, presiding over the end of the fight for Ar Raqqah, the clearance of the last ISIS strongholds in Iraq, and the liberation of all but a few square kilometers still under the rule of the Islamic State.[309]

The ISIS forces in the Hajin pocket put up unexpectedly fierce resistance. Around 5,000 militants, including roughly 2,000 foreign fighters, fought bitterly for every square meter of the caliphate's dwindling territory.[310] The terrorist group even staged a local counterattack on 24 November, breaking out of Hajin and threatening SDF positions in the nearby village of Kharayij (Gharanij).[311] To support the SDF's advance, the coalition launched almost 1,300 airstrikes on targets in the Hajin pocket during the last quarter of 2018, transforming the town and its environs—at that point inhabited almost exclusively by ISIS militants and their families—into a shell-pocked wasteland.[312] Following a prolonged battle, Hajin finally fell to the SDF on 14 December.

The caliphate proved resilient even in its death throes. After it helped capture Hajin, the YPG confidently predicted that it would be able to liberate the final areas of ISIS control "in the next day or two."[313] In fact, it took until March 2019 before the last ISIS enclave, a 4-square-kilometer area nestled along the Iraqi border, finally fell to the SDF—once again with extensive support from coalition airpower.[314] In the midst of this fighting, moreover, the Islamic State carried out the deadliest single attack on CJTF-OIR personnel since the beginning of the campaign. On 16 January 2019, an ISIS suicide bomber approached a restaurant in Manbij, where several Americans were meeting with local defense forces, and detonated an explosive vest. Nineteen people died in the resulting blast, including four members of CJTF-OIR: CWO2 Jonathan R. Farmer; SCPO Shannon M. Kent; Scott A. Wirtz, an employee of the Defense Intelligence Agency; and Ghadir Taher, an Arabic interpreter contracted with the Department of Defense.[315] Taking place in a city that coalition forces had helped to liberate more than two years before, the bombing offered stark proof of the Islamic State's ability to carry out attacks outside of its territorial base.

The end of the caliphate as a territorial entity nevertheless marked a turning point in the coalition's campaign. On 23 March, President Trump proclaimed that the United States and its allies had "liberated all ISIS-controlled territory in Syria and Iraq, 100 percent of the 'caliphate.'"[316] At that time, CJTF-OIR was already withdrawing troops and equipment from Syria. By July, only a residual U.S. presence remained in the country, split between At Tanf in the southeast and the SDF's territory in the northeast.[317]

Events in late 2019 and early 2020 cast the future of Operation INHERENT RESOLVE into doubt. In early October, President Trump directed CJTF-OIR—headed, since September, by now Lt. Gen. Robert P. White, commanding the III Corps—to withdraw fully from northeast Syria.[318] However, the Trump administration quickly reversed course, citing the need to protect the Syrian oil fields. Additional American units, including elements of the 30th Armored Brigade Combat Team, North Carolina Army National Guard, deployed to the country by early November.[319] Coalition special operations forces also continued to carry out direct action missions targeting ISIS's leadership—including an operation in Idlib Province that resulted in the death of the Islamic State's

76

self-styled caliph, Abu Bakr al-Baghdadi, on 26 October.[320] In light of these events, it was unclear at the beginning of 2020 when—or whether—the U.S. government would implement its plans for a complete withdrawal from Syria.[321]

At the same time, the future of the American presence in Iraq was also uncertain. On 3 January 2020, U.S. forces carried out a drone strike on Baghdad International Airport, killing Iranian General Qassem Soleimani and the deputy head of the PMF, Abu Mahdi al-Muhandis. Days later, a majority in the Iraqi parliament, consisting mainly of Shi'a lawmakers, passed a nonbinding resolution requesting a total withdrawal of American troops from Iraq. Whether the Iraqi government would act on the resolution remained to be seen.[322] In the meantime, Operation INHERENT RESOLVE continued, as coalition forces in Iraq and Syria executed their ongoing mission to promote regional stability and ensure the lasting defeat of the Islamic State.

ANALYSIS

On the surface, Operation INHERENT RESOLVE appeared to be a continuation of the conflict that began with Operation IRAQI FREEDOM in 2003. The Islamic State was a successor to AQI. Many of the battlefields of Operation INHERENT RESOLVE were the same as those of the last war. Even the personalities were the same. Generals Pittard, MacFarland, Townsend, Funk, LaCamera, and White had all served in Iraq at various times between 2003 and 2011, as had many of their subordinates. Likewise, many ISIS combatants were former insurgents who had fought U.S. and Iraqi government forces before 2011.

These superficial similarities belied more significant differences. Fundamentally, neither the United States nor the Islamic State approached the new conflict using the methods of the last war: ISIS did not fight primarily as an insurgency, and the United States did not wage a counterinsurgency campaign. The Islamic State's early victories in the Sunni regions of Iraq and Syria won the group immense prestige and enabled it to proclaim that it had reestablished the caliphate. Paradoxically, these same victories also represented a serious liability. The very prestige that ISIS derived from its conquests compelled it to defend its territory, including urban centers like Mosul. This meant that it could not rely primarily on the insurgent tactics

A Mine-Resistant Ambush Protected Vehicle (MRAP) is loaded onto a C–17 Globemaster III during the U.S. forces' withdrawal from Syria, 24 October 2019. (*U.S. Army Reserve*)

that had propelled it to prominence in the first place. Instead, when U.S. forces intervened in Iraq in the summer of 2014, ISIS was well on its way toward transforming itself from an insurgent group into a conventional military force. The newly established caliphate fielded semiregular military formations and held fixed positions on the battlefield, usually to defend cities. ISIS therefore forfeited its ability to use its most-favored style of warfare and was forced to switch to one in which its opponents— particularly the Iraqi government and the United States—held many advantages.

The U.S. Army likewise approached the war in a new way. The Obama administration was adamant from the beginning that American combat troops would not deploy to Iraq to fight the Islamic State on the ground, and the Trump administration never really deviated from this principle. The U.S.-led campaign against ISIS consequently relied on an indirect approach, in which support for local partners or proxies—the ISF, the SDF, and the Peshmerga—was the main effort. This support came in three main forms: an air campaign, involving both bombing and reconnaissance; a train-and-equip mission intended to enhance existing partner force units and to generate new ones; and a military advisory effort focused on assisting all partner echelons from defense ministries down to brigades and battalions. Within the U.S. military, the general phrase used for this method, as it evolved during the campaign, was the "by-with-through" operational approach. This entailed operations "led *by* our [U.S.] partners, state or nonstate, *with* enabling support from the United States or U.S.-led coalitions, and *through* U.S. authorities and partner agreements."[323] The by-with-through approach applied mainly to ground operations; air support remained primarily under direct coalition control, with the Iraqi Air Force playing a relatively minor role.

Each dimension of the coalition effort contributed to the successful outcome of the campaign. In the first place, airstrikes proved highly valuable in halting ISIS's offensive momentum and creating space for the ISF to regroup. Aerial surveillance gave U.S. forces an unparalleled view of the battlefield, making it difficult for ISIS forces to operate in the open. Less than a month after the first U.S. airstrikes in Iraq, the Islamic State began to scale back its use of the kind of massed formations that had proved so successful against the ISF and Peshmerga during the summer of 2014. The assault on Kobani was the Islamic State's last real attempt to launch a conventional attack on a ground force backed by coalition airpower. After its defeat in that battle, ISIS succeeded on the offensive only when it either targeted the Syrian regime or took advantage of adverse weather conditions that limited the effectiveness of air support. Otherwise, it shifted over to the strategic defensive, undertaking only limited counterattacks.

While on the defensive, the Islamic State fought primarily in cities, where dense urban terrain and the presence of civilians afforded some protection from aerial attack. Even so, airpower continued to degrade ISIS's effectiveness, killing thousands of militants and disrupting its lucrative oil production and smuggling operations. But airstrikes on their own were insufficient to ensure the Islamic State's final defeat; it was still necessary for ground forces to attack and liberate the caliphate's territory. In 2014, however, neither the ISF nor the Peshmerga were able to defeat ISIS on the battlefield. The only Iraqi military organizations that showed real offensive capability were the CTS—an elite force that was too small to fight ISIS on its own—and the PMF—a Shi'a-dominated organization that might do more harm than good in light of Iraq's sectarian tensions. Training, equipping, and advising the ISF, the SDF, and the Peshmerga consequently formed a key part of the coalition's campaign.

The U.S. military had garnered extensive experience performing these missions in support of Iraqi forces between 2003 and 2011, but this earlier involvement did not fully prepare American units for their task during Operation INHERENT RESOLVE. As one U.S. brigade commander noted, his unit's mission "proved infinitely different than the exhausting, firsthand combat that many of us experienced in Iraq from 2003 to 2008," when the "typical American soldier's experience . . . was that Americans did the deadliest work, as Iraqis observed." In 2017, by contrast, "the entire effort always centered on our partners' leadership and ownership of exceptionally nasty ground combat operations." The absence of U.S. combat troops on the ground ensured that the ISF and SDF truly were in the lead. Coalition advisers could only propose courses of action and provide support.[324]

At times, this hands-off arrangement could be frustrating, as partner forces did not always act in accordance with the U.S. military's standard operating procedures. The Iraqi Army, for example, approached logistics in a way that struck some Americans as wrong-headed. Rather than anticipating shortages and planning supply shipments ahead of time, the Iraqis tended to operate until they ran out of an essential item—like ammunition or fuel—and then request resupply. Their forces would then halt while they rested and refitted. As one U.S. officer commented, "We've seen time and again where they'll do that pause and that gives the enemy that time to reset. That makes the next phase harder again. Whereas we [Americans] would see our foot on the throat and [that] now is the time to take the advantage[,] but that's not something they [the Iraqis] necessarily do."[325] Coalition forces only had so much leverage over their partners. As one report noted, CJTF-OIR "had no sticks, only carrots to offer or deny."[326]

The consequences of the coalition's lack of control over its partners' ground operations were mixed. The ISF's idiosyncrasies, including its leaders' habit of alternating between brief periods of aggressive maneuver and lengthy operational pauses, may have prolonged the campaign unnecessarily. The extreme duration of the battles for Ar Ramadi and Mosul—roughly nine months in each case—was the result, in part, of the ISF's irregular operational tempo. Meanwhile, the Iraqis' overreliance on certain elite formations to do most of the hard fighting also had adverse effects. In East Mosul, for example, the Iraqi Task Force CTS wore itself out leading attack after attack, suffering roughly 50 percent casualties. This overuse led to a sustained drop in the skill level of the ISF's most capable force and reduced the CTS, at least temporarily, to near combat-ineffectiveness.[327] Finally, the SDF's willingness to negotiate with the Islamic State without informing the coalition created a distinct set of problems. By allowing defeated ISIS forces to escape from Al Tabaqah and Ar Raqqah, the SDF ensured that veteran militants would live to fight another day. Per one U.S. report, "'Surrendering' under arms with the intent to rejoin battle at a later date is not surrender, it is a force preservation measure."[328] However, none of these practices precluded the coalition's success on the battlefield.

More consequential, potentially, was CJTF-OIR's inability to prevent its partners from carrying out reprisals against defeated populations. Reports of atrocities followed the coalition victories at Amirli, Tikrit, Al Fallujah, and elsewhere.[329] Sectarian violence against Sunni Iraqis in particular threatened to undermine the entire campaign against ISIS. As the coalition leaders recognized from the beginning, victory over the Islamic State entailed more than just defeating the terrorist group on the battlefield. It was necessary to eliminate the kind of abuses that led ISIS to become popular in the first place.

Ultimately, however, CJTF-OIR succeeded in its primary mission. As of September 2021, the Islamic State remains a shadow of its former self—at least in its heartland in Iraq and Syria. Although it continues to pose a threat and may rise again, its position now is comparable to that of AQI in 2010. The by-with-through approach to fighting the Islamic State obviated the need for a deployment of U.S. combat troops, reduced the financial cost of the campaign, and kept coalition casualties to a minimum. But the sacrifices required to defeat ISIS, including the fifteen coalition servicemen and servicewomen killed in action during the period of active combat operations, were nonetheless real. Counting noncombat fatalities, seventy-six U.S. members of CJTF-OIR lost their lives between the initial intervention in June 2014 and the fall of the territorial caliphate in March 2019.[330]

NOTES

1. Moni Basu, "Deadly Iraq War Ends with Exit of Last U.S. Troops," CNN, 18 Dec 2011, https://www.cnn.com/2011/12/17/world/meast/iraq-troops-leave/index.html, Historians Files, U.S. Army Center of Military History, Washington, DC (hereinafter cited as Hist Files, CMH).

2. Barack H. Obama and Michelle L. R. Obama, "Remarks by the President and First Lady on the End of the War in Iraq" (speech, Fort Bragg, NC, 14 Dec 2011), https://obamawhitehouse.archives.gov/the-press-office/2011/12/14/remarks-president-and-first-lady-end-war-iraq, Hist Files, CMH.

3. Seth G. Jones et al., *Rolling Back the Islamic State* (Santa Monica, CA: RAND Corporation, 2017), xi.

4. U.S. Central Intelligence Agency (CIA), "Iraq," in *The World Factbook 2014* (Washington, DC: Central Intelligence Agency, 2014), https://www.cia.gov/the-world-factbook/about/archives, Hist Files, CMH.

5. Jourden Travis Moger, *Between Desert Storm and Iraqi Freedom: U.S. Army Operations in the Middle East, 1991–2001* (Washington, DC: U.S. Army Center of Military History, 2021).

6. See Joel D. Rayburn and Frank K. Sobchack, eds., *The U.S. Army in the Iraq War*, 2 vol. (Carlisle Barracks, PA: U.S. Army War College Press, 2019).

7. Nicholas J. Schlosser, *The Surge, 2007–2008*, U.S. Army Campaigns in Iraq (Washington, DC: U.S. Army Center of Military History, 2017); Rayburn and Sobchack, *The U.S. Army in the Iraq War*, vol. 2, *Surge and Withdrawal, 2007–2011*, 502–5.

8. Katelyn K. Tietzen, *Transition and Withdrawal: The U.S. Army in Operation IRAQI FREEDOM and Operation NEW DAWN, 2009–2011*, U.S. Army Campaigns in Iraq (Washington, DC: U.S Army Center of Military History, forthcoming).

9. Rayburn and Sobchack, *U.S. Army in the Iraq War*, 2:569–71, 2:576–79.

10. Rick Brennan Jr. et al., *Ending the U.S. War in Iraq: The Final Transition, Operational Maneuver, and Disestablishment of United States Forces–Iraq* (Santa Monica, CA: RAND Corporation, 2013), 171–72, 310; Eric Schmitt and Michael R. Gordon, "The Iraqi Army Was Crumbling Long Before Its Collapse, U.S. Officials Say," *New York Times*, 12 Jun 2014, https://www.nytimes.com/2014/06/13/world/middleeast/american-intelligence-officials-said-iraqi-military-had-been-in-decline.html, Hist Files, CMH.

11. Rayburn and Sobchack, *U.S. Army in the Iraq War*, 2:571–76; Brennan et al., *Ending the U.S. War in Iraq*, 169–71; U.S. Dept. of Def Inspector Gen (DoDIG), *Assessment of the Office of Security Cooperation–Iraq Mission Capabilities*, 18 Sep 2013, i, 13–18, https://www.dodig.mil/reports.html/article/1118974/assessment-of-the-office-of-security-cooperation-iraq-mission-capabilities/, Hist Files, CMH.

12. Prepared Statement, James N. Mattis, *Department of Defense Authorization for Appropriations for Fiscal Year 2013 and the Future Years Defense Program: Hearings Before the Committee on Armed Services, United States Senate*, 112th Cong. (14, 28 Feb, 1, 6, 8, 13, 15, 20, 27 Mar 2012), 396, https://www.govinfo.gov/content/pkg/CHRG-112shrg76537/pdf/CHRG-112shrg76537.pdf, Hist Files, CMH.

13. Olga Khazan, "Who's Fighting Whom in Syria?," *Washington Post*, 18 Oct 2012, https://www.washingtonpost.com/news/worldviews/wp/2012/10/18/whos-fighting-who-in-syria/, Hist Files, CMH. Sources differ on the precise ethno-religious composition of the population. See, for example, CIA, "Syria," in *The World Factbook 2011* (Washington, DC: Central Intelligence Agency, 2011), https://www.cia.gov/the-world-factbook/about/archives, Hist Files, CMH.

14. William Harris, *Quicksilver War: Syria, Iraq and the Spiral of Conflict* (New York: Oxford University Press, 2018), 26–33; Christopher Phillips, *The Battle for Syria: International Rivalry in the New Middle East* (New Haven, CT: Yale University Press, 2018), 118.

15. Phillips, *Battle for Syria*, 126–29, 137–40.

16. Phillips, *Battle for Syria*, 111; Robin Yassin-Kassab and Leila Al-Shami, *Burning Country: Syrians in Revolution and War*, 2nd ed. (London: Pluto Press, 2018), 73–76; Adam Baczko, Gilles Dorronsoro, and Arthur Quesnay, *Civil War in Syria: Mobilization and Competing Social Orders* (Cambridge, UK: Cambridge University Press, 2018), 164–72.

17. Rayburn and Sobchack, *U.S. Army in the Iraq War*, 2:537–38.

18. Charles R. Lister, *The Syrian Jihad: Al-Qaeda, the Islamic State and the Evolution of an Insurgency* (New York: Oxford University Press, 2015), 55–56.

19. Charles Lister, *Profiling Jabhat al-Nusra*, Brookings Project on U.S. Relations with the Islamic World Analysis Paper No. 24 (Washington, DC: Brookings Institution, 2016).

20. Rayburn and Sobchack, *U.S. Army in the Iraq War*, 2:585–86.

21. Jessica D. Lewis, *Al-Qaeda in Iraq Resurgent: The Breaking the Walls Campaign, Part I*, Middle East Security Rpt 14 (Washington, DC: Institute for the Study of War, 2013).

22. Lister, *Syrian Jihad*, 112–13, 122, 148; Jessica D. Lewis, "AQI's 'Soldiers' Harvest' Campaign," Institute for the Study of War (ISW), 9 Oct 2013, https://understandingwar.org/backgrounder/aqis-soldiers-harvest-campaign, Hist Files, CMH.

23. Rayburn and Sobchack, *U.S. Army in the Iraq War*, 2:582–84; Anthony H. Cordesman and Sam Khazai, *Iraq in Crisis* (New York: Center for Strategic and International Studies, 2014), 1.

24. Kamal Namaa, "Iraqi Militants Kill at Least 18 Soldiers, Including

Commander," Reuters, 20 Dec 2013, https://www.reuters.com/article/us-iraq-violence-idUSBRE9BJ1BA20131221, Hist Files, CMH.

25. Rayburn and Sobchack, *U.S. Army in the Iraq War*, 2:592.

26. Liz Sly, "Al-Qaeda Force Captures Fallujah Amid Rise in Violence in Iraq," *Washington Post*, 3 Jan 2014, https://www.washingtonpost.com/world/al-qaeda-force-captures-fallujah-amid-rise-in-violence-in-iraq/2014/01/03/8abaeb2a-74aa-11e3-8def-a33011492df2_story.html, Hist Files, CMH.

27. Rayburn and Sobchack, *U.S. Army in the Iraq War*, 2:593.

28. Harris, *Quicksilver War*, 50; Lister, *Syrian Jihad*, 234.

29. Testimony, Brett H. McGurk, *Al-Qaeda's Resurgence in Iraq: A Threat to U.S. Interests: Hearing Before the Committee on Foreign Affairs, House of Representatives*, 113th Cong. (5 Feb 2014), 16, https://www.govinfo.gov/content/pkg/CHRG-113hhrg86588/pdf/CHRG-113hhrg86588.pdf, Hist Files, CMH.

30. DoDIG, *Assessment of the Office of Security Cooperation–Iraq Mission Capabilities*, 25.

31. Interv, Mark R. Reardon, CMH, with Lt. Gen. (Ret.) John M. "Mick" Bednarek, former Commanding Gen   (CG), Ofc of Security Cooperation–Iraq (OSC-I), 9 Apr 2019, Hist Files, CMH.

32. Prepared Statement, Brett H. McGurk, *U.S. Foreign Policy Toward Iraq: Hearing Before the Subcommittee on the Middle East and North Africa of the Committee on Foreign Affairs*, 113th Cong. (13 Nov 2013), 16–18, https://www.govinfo.gov/content/pkg/CHRG-113hhrg85554/pdf/CHRG-113hhrg85554.pdf, Hist Files, CMH.

33. Jennifer Epstein, "Obama, Iraqi Leader Talk on Al Qaeda," *Politico*, 1 Nov 2013, https://www.politico.com/story/2013/11/barack-obama-nouri-al-maliki-al-qaeda-iraq-099246, Hist Files, CMH; "U.S. Sends Hellfire Missiles to Iraq," *USA Today*, 27 Dec 2013, https://www.usatoday.com/story/news/world/2013/12/26/us-iraq-missiles-war/4208837/, Hist Files, CMH.

34. Prepared Statement, McGurk, *U.S. Foreign Policy Toward Iraq* (13 Nov 2013), 17, 23–24.

35. Testimony, McGurk, *Al-Qaeda's Resurgence in Iraq* (5 Feb 2014), 19.

36. Prepared Statement, McGurk, *U.S. Foreign Policy Toward Iraq* (13 Nov 2013), 17.

37. Loveday Morris, "Interview with Iraqi Prime Minister Nouri al-Maliki: Transcript," *Washington Post*, 16 Jan 2014, https://www.washingtonpost.com/world/middle_east/interview-with-iraqi-prime-minister-nouri-al-maliki-transcript/2014/01/16/fdf602c0-7eda-11e3-93c1-0e888170b723_story.html, Hist Files, CMH.

38. John F. Kerry, "Remarks at Solo Press Availability" (remarks, Jerusalem, 5 Jan 2014), https://2009-2017.state.gov/secretary/remarks/2014/01/219298.htm,

Hist Files, CMH.

39. Morris, "Interview with Iraqi Prime Minister Nouri al-Maliki."

40. Rayburn and Sobchack, *U.S. Army in the Iraq War*, 2:594.

41. Yasir Abbas and Dan Trombly, "Inside the Collapse of the Iraqi Army's 2nd Division," War on the Rocks, 1 Jul 2014, https://warontherocks. com/2014/07/inside-the-collapse-of-the-iraqi-armys-2nd-division/, Hist Files, CMH; Ned Parker, Isabel Coles, and Raheem Salman, "Special Report: How Mosul Fell – An Iraqi General Disputes Baghdad's Story," Reuters, 14 Oct 2014, https://www.reuters.com/article/us-mideast-crisis-gharawi-special-report-idUSKCN0I30Z820141014, Hist Files, CMH; Prepared Statement, Brett H. McGurk, *Iraq at a Crossroads: Options for U.S. Policy: Hearing Before the Committee on Foreign Relations, United States Senate*, 113th Cong. (24 Jul 2014), 7–8, https://www.govinfo.gov/content/pkg/CHRG-113shrg94805/pdf/CHRG-113shrg94805.pdf, Hist Files, CMH.

42. Barack H. Obama, "Statement by the President on Iraq" (statement, Washington, DC, 13 Jun 2014), https://obamawhitehouse.archives.gov/the-press-office/2014/06/13/statement-president-iraq, Hist Files, CMH.

43. Dana J. H. Pittard and Wes J. Bryant, *Hunting the Caliphate: America's War on ISIS and the Dawn of the Strike Cell* (New York: Post Hill Press, 2019), 80–82.

44. Pittard and Bryant, *Hunting the Caliphate*, 64; David Jackson et al., "Obama Is Sending 275 U.S. Forces to Iraq for Embassy Security," *USA Today*, 16 Jun 2014, https://www.usatoday.com/story/news/world/2014/06/16/iraq-insurgency/10569133/, Hist Files, CMH.

45. "Iraq Conflict: ISIS Militants Seize New Towns," BBC News, 13 Jun 2014, https://www.bbc.com/news/world-middle-east-27828595, Hist Files, CMH.

46. Christoph Wilcke, "Dispatches: Remembering ISIS's Bloodiest Massacre in Iraq," Human Rights Watch, 11 Jun 2015, https://www.hrw.org/news/2015/06/11/dispatches-remembering-isiss-bloodiest-massacre-iraq, Hist Files, CMH; "Iraq Crisis: UN 'Deplores' Militants' Capture of Cities," BBC News, 12 Jun 2014, https://www.bbc.com/news/world-middle-east-27806094, Hist Files, CMH.

47. Prepared Statement, McGurk, *Iraq at a Crossroads* (24 July 2014), 5.

48. Pittard and Bryant, *Hunting the Caliphate*, 71.

49. Ben Van Heuvelen, "Amid Turmoil, Iraq's Kurdish Region Is Laying Foundation for Independent State," *Washington Post*, 12 Jun 2014, https://www.washingtonpost.com/world/middle_east/amid-turmoil-iraqs-kurdish-region-is-laying-foundation-for-independent-state/2014/06/12/c1f22d7c-f26a-11e3-bf76-447a5df6411f_story.html, Hist Files, CMH.

50. Lister, *Syrian Jihad*, 236–41.

51. Press Bfg, Joshua R. H. Earnest, "Press Briefing by Press Secretary Josh

Earnest, 6/23/2014," 23 Jun 2014, https://obamawhitehouse.archives.gov/the-press-office/2014/06/23/press-briefing-press-secretary-josh-earnest-6232014, Hist Files, CMH; Peter Baker, "Diplomatic Notes Promises Immunity from Iraqi Law for U.S. Advisory Troops," *New York Times*, 23 Jun 2014, https://www.nytimes.com/2014/06/24/world/middleeast/us-advisory-troops-get-immunity-from-iraqi-law.html, Hist Files, CMH.

52. Combined Joint Task Force–Opn INHERENT RESOLVE (CJTF-OIR) Press Release, "History," n.d., 1, https://www.inherentresolve.mil/Portals/14/Documents/Mission/HISTORY_17OCT2014-JUL2017.pdf?ver=2017-07-22-095806-793 (page discontinued), Hist Files, CMH.

53. "USACENT as a Joint Force HQ in Operation INHERENT RESOLVE" (unpublished paper, U.S. Army Central [ARCENT], n.d.), Hist Files, CMH.

54. Pittard and Bryant, *Hunting the Caliphate*, 61–62.

55. Telecons, author with Maj. Gen. (Ret.) Dana J. H. Pittard, 4 and 9 Dec 2020, Hist Files, CMH; Pittard and Bryant, *Hunting the Caliphate*, 122.

56. Eric Schmitt and Michael R. Gordon, "U.S. Sees Risks in Assisting a Compromised Iraqi Force," *New York Times*, 14 Jul 2014, https://www.nytimes.com/2014/07/14/world/middleeast/us-sees-risks-in-assisting-a-compromised-iraqi-force.html, Hist Files, CMH.

57. Rayburn and Sobchack, *U.S. Army in the Iraq War*, 2:597.

58. Nader Uskowi, *Temperature Rising: Iran's Revolutionary Guards and Wars in the Middle East* (New York: Rowman & Littlefield, 2019), 101–2.

59. Pittard and Bryant, *Hunting the Caliphate*, 73, 98.

60. Tim Arango, "Jihadists Rout Kurds in North and Seize Strategic Iraqi Dam," *New York Times*, 7 Aug 2014, https://www.nytimes.com/2014/08/08/world/middleeast/isis-forces-in-iraq.html, Hist Files, CMH; Liz Sly, Craig Whitlock, and Loveday Morris, "Kurdish Forces Close in on Mosul Dam, Aided by U.S. Attacks," *Toronto Star*, 17 Aug 2014, https://www.thestar.com/news/world/2014/08/17/kurdish_forces_retake_parts_of_mosul_dam_from_islamic_state_iraqi_official_says.html, Hist Files, CMH.

61. Dexter Filkins, "The Fight of Their Lives," *New Yorker*, 22 Sep 2014, https://www.newyorker.com/magazine/2014/09/29/fight-lives, Hist Files, CMH.

62. Jessica D. Lewis and ISW Iraq Team, "Iraq Situation Report: August 3, 2014," ISW, 3 Aug 2014, https://understandingwar.org/backgrounder/iraq-situation-report-august-3-2014, Hist Files, CMH.

63. Barack H. Obama, "Statement by the President" (statement, Washington, DC, 7 Aug 2014), https://obamawhitehouse.archives.gov/the-press-office/2014/08/07/statement-president, Hist Files, CMH.

64. Dept. of Def (DoD) News Bfg, R. Adm. John F. Kirby, 7 Aug 2014, https://www.defense.gov/News/Releases/Release/Article/605127/statement-by-

pentagon-press-secretary-rear-admiral-john-kirby-on-airstrikes-in/, Hist Files, CMH; DoD News Bfg, R. Adm. John F. Kirby, 8 Aug 2014, https://www.defense. gov/News/Releases/Release/Article/605128/statement-by-pentagon-press-secretary-rear-admiral-john-kirby/, Hist Files, CMH.

65. 35th Fighter Wing Press Release, Benjamin W. Stratton, "Misawa Pilots Save Iraqi Civilians, Earn 2014 Mackay Trophy," 15 Dec 2015, https://www. af.mil/News/Article-Display/Article/634210/misawa-pilots-save-iraqi-civilians-earn-2014-mackay-trophy/, Hist Files, CMH.

66. U.S. Central Cmd (CENTCOM) Press Release #20140807, "Update on Humanitarian Assistance Operations Near Sinjar Iraq," 10 Aug 2014, https://www. centcom.mil/MEDIA/PRESS-RELEASES/Press-Release-View/Article/904088/ update-on-humanitarian-assistance-operations-near-sinjar-iraq/, Hist Files, CMH.

67. Telecon, author with Pittard, 4 Dec 2020; Barack H. Obama, "Statement by the President" (statement, Edgartown, MA, 14 Aug 2014), https:// obamawhitehouse.archives.gov/the-press-office/2014/08/14/statement-president, Hist Files, CMH.

68. Pittard and Bryant, *Hunting the Caliphate*, 126; Alessandro Annunziato, Ioannis Andredakis, and Pamela Probst, *Impact of Flood by a Possible Failure of the Mosul Dam* (Luxembourg: Publications Office of the European Union, 2016), 14–15, https://ec.europa.eu/jrc/en/publication/impact-flood-possible-failure-mosul-dam, Hist Files, CMH.

69. Pittard and Bryant, *Hunting the Caliphate*, 131–33; DoD Press Release, "Statement from Pentagon Press Secretary Rear Admiral John Kirby," 18 Aug 2014, https://www.defense.gov/News/Releases/Release/Article/605139/ statement-from-pentagon-press-secretary-rear-admiral-john-kirby/, Hist Files, CMH; Becca Wasser et al., *The Air War Against the Islamic State: The Role of Airpower in Operation Inherent Resolve* (Santa Monica, CA: RAND Corporation, 2021), 136–39.

70. "Iraq: UN Envoy Calls for Immediate Action to Avert Possible 'Massacre' in Northern Town," UN (United Nations) News, 23 Aug 2014, https://news. un.org/en/story/2014/08/475762-iraq-un-envoy-calls-immediate-action-avert-possible-massacre-northern-town, Hist Files, CMH.

71. Pittard and Bryant, *Hunting the Caliphate*, 143–46; Telecon, author with Pittard, 9 Dec 2020; Isabel Coles, "Iranians Play Role in Breaking IS Siege of Iraqi Town," Reuters, 1 Sep 2014, https://www.reuters.com/article/us-iraq-security-miltias-iran-idUSKBN0GW2Y420140901, Hist Files, CMH; Zeke J. Miller, "Iraqi Forces Break ISIS Siege After U.S. Air Campaign," *Time*, 31 Aug 2014, https://time.com/3233570/iraq-amerli-isis-shiite-turkmen/, Hist Files, CMH.

72. Jim Sciutto, Jamie Crawford, and Chelsea J. Carter, "ISIS Can 'Muster' Between 20,000 and 31,500 Fighters, CIA Says," CNN, 12 Sep 2014, https://

edition.cnn.com/2014/09/11/world/meast/isis-syria-iraq/index.html, Hist Files, CMH.

73. DoD News Bfg, Sec Def Charles T. Hagel and Chairman, Joint Chs of Staff (CJCS) Gen. Martin E. Dempsey, 21 Aug 2014, https://www.defense.gov/News/Transcripts/Transcript/Article/606917/department-of-defense-press-briefing-by-secretary-hagel-and-general-dempsey-in/, Hist Files, CMH.

74. Barack H. Obama and Toomas H. Ilves, "Remarks by President Obama and President Ilves of Estonia in Joint Press Conference" (remarks, Tallinn, Estonia, 3 Sep 2014), https://obamawhitehouse.archives.gov/the-press-office/2014/09/03/remarks-president-obama-and-president-ilves-estonia-joint-press-confer-0, Hist Files, CMH.

75. Barack H. Obama, "Statement by the President on ISIL" (remarks, Washington, DC, 10 Sep 2014), https://obamawhitehouse.archives.gov/the-press-office/2014/09/10/statement-president-isil-1, Hist Files, CMH.

76. John F. Kerry, "Remarks at Top of Meeting on Building an Anti-ISIL Coalition Co-Chaired by Defense Secretary Chuck Hagel, U.K. Foreign Secretary Philip Hammond, and U.K. Defense Secretary Michael Fallon" (remarks, Newport, UK, 5 Sep 2014), https://2009-2017.state.gov/secretary/remarks/2014/09/231288.htm, Hist Files, CMH; Barack H. Obama, "Remarks by President Obama at NATO Summit Press Conference" (remarks, Newport, UK, 5 Sep 2014), https://obamawhitehouse.archives.gov/the-press-office/2014/09/05/remarks-president-obama-nato-summit-press-conference, Hist Files, CMH; John F. Kerry, "Announcement of General John Allen as Special Presidential Envoy for the Global Coalition to Counter ISIL" (statement, Washington, DC, 13 Sep 2014), https://2009-2017.state.gov/secretary/remarks/2014/09/231627.htm, Hist Files, CMH.

77. Dept. of State (DoS) Press Release, "Building International Support to Counter ISIL," 19 Sep 2014, https://2009-2017.state.gov/r/pa/prs/ps/2014/09/231886.htm, Hist Files, CMH; Loveday Morris, "French Fighter Jets Strike Islamic State Supply Depot in Northeastern Iraq," *Washington Post*, 19 Sep 2014, https://www.washingtonpost.com/world/french-fighter-jets-strike-islamic-state-supply-depot-in-northeastern-iraq/2014/09/19/d260dda7-330c-4c86-a24b-658158f6b0ed_story.html, Hist Files, CMH; Dan Lamothe, "U.S. and Britain Combine to Launch the Largest Day Yet for Airstrikes in Iraq and Syria," *Washington Post*, 30 Sep 2014, https://www.washingtonpost.com/news/checkpoint/wp/2014/09/30/u-s-and-britain-combine-to-launch-the-largest-day-yet-for-airstrikes-in-iraq-and-syria/, Hist Files, CMH.

78. John Kerry, *Every Day Is Extra* (New York: Simon & Schuster, 2018), 543–44.

79. Barack H. Obama and Haider al-Abadi, "Remarks by President Obama and

Prime Minister Abadi of the Republic of Iraq After Bilateral Meeting" (remarks, New York, NY, 24 Sep 2014), https://obamawhitehouse.archives.gov/the-press-office/2014/09/24/remarks-president-obama-and-prime-minister-abadi-republic-iraq-after-bil, Hist Files, CMH.

80. Obama, "Statement by the President on ISIL," 10 Sep 2014.

81. Making Continuing Appropriations for Fiscal Year 2015, and for Other Purposes, PL 113–164, 128 Stat. 1867 (2014), 1874–75; Lead Inspector Gen for Overseas Contingency Opns (LIG-OCO), *Operation Inherent Resolve: October 1, 2015–December 31, 2015*, Rpt to Cong., 16 Feb 2016, 46, https://www.dodig.mil/Reports/Lead-Inspector-General-Reports/Article/1159953/lead-inspector-general-for-operation-inherent-resolve-quarterly-report-to-the-u/, Hist Files, CMH; Ben Jacobs and Sabrina Siddiqui, "US Begins Training Syrian Rebels in Jordan to Become Anti-Isis Force," *Guardian*, 7 May 2015, https://www.theguardian.com/world/2015/may/07/us-begins-training-syrian-rebels-jordan-anti-isis-force, Hist Files, CMH.

82. DoD News Bfg, Lt. Gen. William C. Mayville Jr., Director of Opns, Joint Staff, and R. Adm. John F. Kirby, DoD Press Sec, 23 Sep 2014, https://www.defense.gov/News/Transcripts/Transcript/Article/606931/department-of-defense-press-briefing-on-operations-in-syria-by-lt-gen-mayville/, Hist Files, CMH.

83. CENTCOM Press Release #20140925, "Sept. 23: U.S. Military, Partner Nations Conduct Airstrikes Against ISIL in Syria," 23 Sep 2014, https://www.centcom.mil/MEDIA/NEWS-ARTICLES/News-Article-View/Article/884858/sept-23-us-military-partner-nations-conduct-airstrikes-against-isil-in-syria/, Hist Files, CMH.

84. Macon Phillips, "President Obama: 'The Future of Syria Must Be Determined by Its People, but President Bashar al-Assad Is Standing in Their Way,'" *White House Blog*, 18 Aug 2011, https://obamawhitehouse.archives.gov/blog/2011/08/18/President-obama-future-syria-must-be-determined-its-people-President-bashar-al-assad, Hist Files, CMH; Margaret Brennan, "U.S. Recognizes Syrian Opposition," CBS News, 11 Dec 2012, https://www.cbsnews.com/news/us-recognizes-syrian-opposition/, Hist Files, CMH.

85. Wasser et al., *Air War Against the Islamic State*, 43, 45–46.

86. AAR, Opn Inherent Resolve, Combined Joint Forces Land Component Cmd–Iraq (CJFLCC-I) and 1st Inf Div, Oct 2014–Jun 2015, 25 Jun 2015, 2, Hist Files, CMH.

87. LIG-OCO, *Operation Inherent Resolve: December 17, 2014–March 31, 2015*, Rpt to Cong., 30 Apr 2015, 12, https://www.dodig.mil/reports.html/Article/1150803/lead-inspector-general-for-operation-inherent-resolve-quarterly-report-and-bian/, Hist Files, CMH; David R. Kogon, *The Sky Dragon*

Dismantles the "Caliphate": The Coalition Military Campaign to Defeat the Islamic State in Iraq and Syria, 21 AUG 2016–05 SEP 2017 (Camp Arifjan, Kuwait: CJTF-OIR HQ, 2017), 8, Hist Files, CMH; Julian E. Barnes, "Operation Name-That-Mission: The Hunt for Military Monikers," *Wall Street Journal*, 3 Oct 2014, https://www.wsj.com/articles/operation-name-that-mission-1412304863, Hist Files, CMH.

88. Center for Army Lessons Learned (CALL) Initial Impressions Rpt 16–10, *ARCENT Transition to Combined Joint Task Force – Operation Inherent Resolve: Lessons and Best Practices* (Fort Leavenworth, KS: Center for Army Lessons Learned, 2016), 5–8, 12, https://usacac.army.mil/sites/default/files/publications/16-10.pdf, Hist Files, CMH.

89. CALL Initial Impression Rpt 16–10, *ARCENT Transition to Combined Joint Task Force – Operation Inherent Resolve*, 12, 14–15; Dean A. Huard, "Sustaining Operation Inherent Resolve," *Army Sustainment* 49, no. 3 (May-Jun 2017): 57; DoDIG, *U.S. and Coalition Efforts to Train, Advise, Assist, and Equip Iraqi Sunni Popular Mobilization Forces*, 29 Feb 2016, 3, https://www.dodig.mil/FOIA/FOIA-Reading-Room/Article/2405208/us-and-coalition-efforts-to-train-advise-assist-and-equip-iraqi-sunni-popular-m/, Hist Files, CMH.

90. Interv, Fred Allison, U.S. Marine Corps (USMC) History Div, with Col. Jason Q. Bohm, former Cdr, Special Purpose Marine Air Ground Task Force–Crisis Response–Central Cmd (SPMAGTF-CR-CC), 12 Aug 2015, Hist Files, CMH; "Q&A: Lt. Gen. Terry," *U.S. Army Central Desert Voice* (Fall 2015), 6, Hist Files, CMH; DoDIG, *U.S. and Coalition Efforts to Train, Advise, Assist, and Equip Iraqi Sunni Popular Mobilization Forces*; DoDIG, *Assessment of U.S. and Coalition Plans and Efforts to Train, Advise, Assist, and Equip the Iraqi Counterterrorism Service and the Iraqi Special Operations Forces*, 19 Apr 2017, https://www.dodig.mil/Reports/Audits-and-Evaluations/Article/1189785/assessment-of-us-and-coalition-plans-and-efforts-to-train-advise-assist-and-equ/, Hist Files, CMH; David M. Witty, *Iraq's Post-2014 Counter Terrorism Service*, Policy Focus 157 (Washington, DC: Washington Institute for Near East Policy, 2018), 51.

91. AAR, Opn INHERENT RESOLVE, CJFLCC-I and 1st Inf Div, 25 Jun 2015, 2; Col. Curtis A. Buzzard, Lt. Col. John C. White, and Maj. Jared N. Ferguson, "An Exercise in Mission Command: The Panther Brigade in Operation Inherent Resolve," *Infantry* 105, no. 2 (Apr-Jul 2016): 33, https://www.benning.army.mil/infantry/magazine/issues/2016/APR-JUL/pdf/A-J16_whole%20mag.pdf, Hist Files, CMH.

92. Wasser et al., *Air War Against the Islamic State*, 351–53.

93. Testimony, Brett H. McGurk, *Countering ISIS: Are We Making Progress? Hearing Before the Committee on Foreign Affairs, House of Representatives*, 113th Cong. (10 Dec 2014), 6, 37, 47, 51–52, 54, 59, https://www.govinfo.gov/

content/pkg/CHRG-113hhrg91843/pdf/CHRG-113hhrg91843.pdf, Hist Files, CMH; Kogon, *Sky Dragon Dismantles the "Caliphate,"* 9.

94. Lister, *Syrian Jihad*, 287; Charlie Caris and Jennifer Cafarella, "Syria Update: September 12–19, 2014," ISW, 19 Sep 2014, https://www.understanding-war.org/backgrounder/syria-update-september-12-19-2014, Hist Files, CMH.

95. Derek Henry Flood, "The Battle for Kobani Comes to the Fore," *CTC Sentinel* 7, no. 11 (Nov-Dec 2014): 5–9, https://ctc.usma.edu/the-battle-for-kobani-comes-to-the-fore/, Hist Files, CMH; Rebecca Grant, "The Siege of Kobani," *Air Force Magazine* 102, no. 10 (Oct-Nov 2018): 38, https://www.airforcemag.com/PDF/MagazineArchive/Magazine%20Documents/2018/October%202018/Air%20Force%20Magazine%20October%202018%20Full%20Issue.pdf, Hist Files, CMH.

96. Grant, "Siege of Kobani," 39.

97. DoD News Bfg, Gen. Lloyd J. Austin III, Combatant Cdr, CENTCOM, 17 Oct 2014, https://www.defense.gov/News/Transcripts/Transcript/Article/606948/department-of-defense-press-briefing-by-general-austin-in-the-pentagon-briefing/, Hist Files, CMH.

98. Wasser et al., *Air War Against the Islamic State*, 142–51.

99. Lister, *Syrian Jihad*, 320; "Battle for Kobane: Key Events," BBC News, 25 Jun 2015, https://www.bbc.com/news/world-middle-east-29688108, Hist Files, CMH.

100. Wladimir van Wilgenburg, "Kobane and the Myth of ISIL Expansion," Al Jazeera, 28 Jan 2015, https://www.aljazeera.com/opinions/2015/1/28/kobane-and-the-myth-of-isil-expansion, Hist Files, CMH. Estimates for ISIS's losses in the battle vary widely. See "After About Four Months of Fighting ISIS Was Defeated in the Kurdish City of Kobani (Ayn al-Arab) in Northern Syria," Israeli Intel Heritage and Commemoration Center, 8 Feb 2015, https://www.terrorism-info.org.il/en/20768/, Hist Files, CMH.

101. Grant, "Siege of Kobani," 41; Kogon, *Sky Dragon Dismantles the "Caliphate,"* 11.

102. Aaron Stein and Michelle Foley, "The YPG-PKK Connection," Atlantic Council, 26 Jan 2016, https://www.atlanticcouncil.org/blogs/menasource/the-ypg-pkk-connection/, Hist Files, CMH.

103. Interv, Allison with Bohm, 12 Aug 2015; AAR, Opn Inherent Resolve, CJFLCC-I and 1st Inf Div, 25 Jun 2015, 59.

104. Tim Arango, "U.S. Troops, Back in Iraq, Train a Force to Fight ISIS," *New York Times*, 31 Dec 2014, https://www.nytimes.com/2014/12/31/world/us-troops-back-in-iraq-train-a-force-to-fight-isis.html, Hist Files, CMH.

105. Buzzard, White, and Ferguson, "An Exercise in Mission Command," 32–33. The authors misidentify the 1st Armored Brigade Combat Team as the 1st

Brigade Combat Team.

106. AAR, Opn Inherent Resolve, CJFLCC-I and 1st Inf Div, 25 Jun 2015, 34. By June, non-U.S. coalition members had already taken the lead in the training mission. See DoDIG, *Assessment of DoD/USCENTCOM and Coalition Plans/Efforts to Train, Advise, and Assist the Iraqi Army to Defeat the Islamic State of Iraq and the Levant*, 30 Sep 2015, 3, https://www.dodig.mil/reports.html/Article/1119206/assessment-of-doduscentcom-and-coalition-plansefforts-to-train-advise-and-assis/, Hist Files, CMH.

107. Victor Hernández, "Cinco años en apoyo de Irak" [Five years of support in Iraq], *Revista Española de Defensa* 33, no. 370 (Mar 2020): 20–21, https://www.defensa.gob.es/Galerias/gabinete/red/2020/03/p-20-25-red-370-irak.pdf, Hist Files, CMH.

108. CJTF-OIR Press Release, "Four Years of Training for Iraqi Troops," 30 Mar 2019, https://www.inherentresolve.mil/Releases/News-Releases/Article/1801091/four-years-of-training-for-iraqi-troops/, Hist Files, CMH.

109. Interv, Allison with Bohm, 12 Aug 2015.

110. See Ahmed Ali and Sinan Adnan, "Iraq Situation Report: December 17–19, 2014," ISW, 19 Dec 2014, http://www.understandingwar.org/backgrounder/iraq-situation-report-december-17-19-2014, Hist Files, CMH; Sinan Adnan, "Iraq Situation Report: December 30–31, 2014," ISW, 31 Dec 2014, https://www.understandingwar.org/backgrounder/iraq-situation-report-december-30-31-2014, Hist Files, CMH; and Sinan Adnan, "Iraq Situation Report January 20–21, 2015," ISW, 21 Jan 2015, https://www.understandingwar.org/backgrounder/iraq-situation-report-january-20-21-2015, Hist Files, CMH. For the relief of Mount Sinjar, see "Mount Sinjar: Islamic State Siege Broken, Say Kurds," BBC News, 19 Dec 2014, https://www.bbc.com/news/world-middle-east-30539170, Hist Files, CMH.

111. Mark Thompson, "U.S. Troops Now Under 'Frequent' Attack at Iraqi Base," *Time*, 5 Jan 2015, https://time.com/3654879/al-asad-iraq-attacks-isis/, Hist Files, CMH.

112. "Islamic State Fighters Seize Western Iraqi Town – Officials," Reuters, 12 Feb 2015, https://www.reuters.com/article/mideast-crisis-iraq-anbar/islamic-state-fighters-seize-western-iraqi-town-officials-idINKBN0LG2NY20150212, Hist Files, CMH.

113. Loveday Morris, "Islamic State Tries to Attack Base Where Hundreds of U.S. Troops Are Stationed," *Washington Post*, 13 Feb 2015, https://www.washingtonpost.com/world/middle_east/islamic-state-tries-to-attack-base-where-hundreds-of-us-troops-are-stationed/2015/02/13/726fcd16-3d8b-42ca-8f09-d44e902ef46f_story.html, Hist Files, CMH; Interv, Allison with Bohm, 12 Aug 2015.

114. DoD News Bfg, CENTCOM Official, 19 Feb 2015, https://www. defense.gov/News/Transcripts/Transcript/Article/607013/department-of-defense-background-briefing-via-teleconference-by-an-official-fro/, Hist Files, CMH; Nick Simeone, "Centcom Official: Mosul Fight Could Begin Within Weeks," DoD News, 19 Feb 2015, http://archive.defense.gov/news/newsarticle.aspx?id=128208 (page discontinued), Hist Files, CMH. See also Ashton B. Carter, *A Lasting Defeat: The Campaign to Destroy ISIS* (Cambridge, MA: Belfer Center for Science and International Affairs, 2017), 13–14, https://www.belfercenter.org/publication/lasting-defeat-campaign-destroy-isis, Hist Files, CMH.

115. Prepared Statement, Lloyd J. Austin III, *Department of Defense Authorization for Appropriations for Fiscal Year 2016 and the Future Years Defense Program: Hearings Before the Committee on Armed Services, United States Senate*, 114th Cong. (3, 10, 12, 18, 19, 26 Mar, 16, 30 Apr 2015), 572, https://www.govinfo.gov/content/pkg/CHRG-114shrg23397/pdf/CHRG-114shrg23397.pdf, Hist Files, CMH.

116. Loveday Morris, "Iraqi Offensive for Tikrit Stalls as Casualties Mount," *Washington Post*, 16 Mar 2016, https://www.washingtonpost.com/world/middle_east/iraqi-offensive-for-tikrit-stalls-as-islamic-state-inflicts-casualties/2015/03/16/258a6dec-cb58-11e4-8730-4f473416e759_story.html, Hist Files, CMH.

117. Rod Nordland and Peter Baker, "Opening New Iraq Front, U.S. Strikes ISIS in Tikrit," *New York Times*, 25 Mar 2015, https://www.nytimes.com/2015/03/26/world/middleeast/iraq-islamic-state-tikrit-united-states-air-strikes.html, Hist Files, CMH.

118. Tim Arango, "Key Iraqi City Falls to ISIS as Last of Security Forces Flee," *New York Times*, 17 May 2015, https://www.nytimes.com/2015/05/18/world/middleeast/isis-ramadi-iraq.html, Hist Files, CMH; DoS Press Bfg, Senior State Dept. Official, 20 May 15, https://2009-2017.state.gov/r/pa/prs/ps/2015/05/242665.htm, Hist Files, CMH; Patrick Martin, Genevieve Casagrande, Jessica Lewis McFate, and the ISW Iraq and Syria Teams, "ISIS Captures Ramadi," ISW, 18 May 2015, https://www.understandingwar.org/backgrounder/isis-captures-ramadi, Hist Files, CMH.

119. Sinan Adnan, "Iraq Situation Report: May 19–20, 2015," ISW, 20 May 2015, https://www.understandingwar.org/backgrounder/iraq-situation-report-may-19-20-2015, Hist Files, CMH; Sinan Adnan, "Iraq Situation Report: May 21–22, 2015," ISW, 22 May 2015, https://www.understandingwar.org/backgrounder/iraq-situation-report-may-21-22-2015, Hist Files, CMH; Josh Lawrence, "Iraq Situation Report: May 23–25, 2015," ISW, 26 May 2015, https://www.understandingwar.org/backgrounder/iraq-situation-report-may-23-25-2015, Hist Files, CMH.

120. Anne Bernard and Hwaida Saad, "ISIS Fighters Seize Control of Syrian City of Palmyra, and Ancient Ruins," *New York Times*, 20 May 2015, https://www. nytimes.com/2015/05/21/world/middleeast/syria-isis-fighters-enter-ancient-city-of-palmyra.html, Hist Files, CMH.

121. Kogon, *Sky Dragon Dismantles the "Caliphate,"* 11.

122. Prepared Statement, Ashton B. Carter, *U.S. Policy and Strategy in the Middle East: Committee on Armed Services, House of Representatives*, 114th Cong. (17 Jun 2015), 6–7, https://www.govinfo.gov/content/pkg/CHRG-114hhrg95315/pdf/CHRG-114hhrg95315.pdf, Hist Files, CMH.

123. USMC Press Release, Ricardo Hurtado, "Iraqi, Coalition Forces Turning Tide in Fight to Defeat ISIL," 1 Apr 2016, http://www.imef.marines.mil/News/News-Article-Display/Article/711256/iraqi-coalition-forces-turning-tide-in-fight-to-defeat-isil/ (page discontinued), Hist Files, CMH.

124. U.S. Army Press Release, William Reinier, "Division Takes Lead of Command in Iraq," 30 Jun 2015, https://www.army.mil/article/151370/division_takes_lead_of_command_in_iraq, Hist Files, CMH.

125. "Iraqi Forces Suffer Casualties as They Advance in Anbar," Al Jazeera, 24 Jul 2015, https://www.aljazeera.com/news/2015/7/24/iraq-forces-suffer-casualties-as-they-advance-in-anbar, Hist Files, CMH; DoD News Bfg, Col Curtis A. Buzzard, Cdr, 3d Bde Combat Team, 82d Abn Div, and Maj. Michael Hamilton, 5 Nov 2015, Defense Visual Information Distribution Service, https://www.dvidshub.net/video/432858/commander-task-force-panther-briefs-operation-inherent-resolve.

126. Loveday Morris, "The Battle to Retake Ramadi Is Going Nowhere," *Washington Post*, 6 Sep 2015, https://www.washingtonpost.com/world/the-battle-to-retake-ramadi-is-going-nowhere/2015/09/03/8e4d4792-4dac-11e5-80c2-106ea7fb80d4_story.html, Hist Files, CMH.

127. Cheryl Cox, "Warrior Brigade Assumes Mission in Iraq," DoD News, 17 Sep 2015, https://www.dvidshub.net/news/176674/warrior-brigade-assumes-mission-iraq, Hist Files, CMH.

128. Donald Sparks, "III Corps Assumes Operation Inherent Resolve Mission," CENTCOM, 22 Sep 2015, https://www.centcom.mil/MEDIA/NEWS-ARTICLES/News-Article-View/Article/885293/iii-corps-assumes-operation-inherent-resolve-mission/, Hist Files, CMH.

129. LIG-OCO, *Operation Inherent Resolve: September 30, 2015*, Rpt to Cong., 25 Nov 2015, 26, https://www.dodig.mil/reports.html/Article/1150786/lead-inspector-general-for-operation-inherent-resolve-quarterly-and-biannual-re/, Hist Files, CMH.

130. Laura Smith-Spark and Noisette Martel, "U.S. Official: 10,000-Plus ISIS Fighters Killed in 9-Month Campaign," CNN, 3 Jun 2015, https://www.cnn.com/2015/06/03/middleeast/isis-conflict/index.html, Hist Files, CMH.

131. DoD News Bfg, Col. Steven Warren, 13 Oct 2015, https://www.defense.gov/News/Transcripts/Transcript/Article/622954/department-of-defense-press-briefing-by-col-warren-via-teleconference-in-the-pe/, Hist Files, CMH.

132. Ltr, Gen. Lloyd J. Austin to Sen. Angus S. King Jr., 9 Nov 2015, in *United States Strategy and Military Operations to Counter the Islamic State in Iraq and the Levant and United States Policy Toward Iraq and Syria: Hearings Before the Committee on Armed Services, United States Senate*, 114th Cong. (21 May, 7 Jul, 16 Sep, 9 Dec 2015), 155–57, https://www.govinfo.gov/content/pkg/CHRG-114shrg21326/pdf/CHRG-114shrg21326.pdf, Hist Files, CMH.

133. Ltr, Austin to King, 9 Nov 2015; see also LIG-OCO, *Operation Inherent Resolve: April 1, 2015–June 30, 2015*, Rpt to Cong., 24 Aug 2015, 21, https://www.dodig.mil/Reports/Lead-Inspector-General-Reports/Article/1150793/2015-lead-inspector-general-for-overseas-contingency-operations-operation-inher/, Hist Files, CMH.

134. Kogon, *Sky Dragon Dismantles the "Caliphate,"* 11.

135. Unclassified redaction of Francis J. H. Park, *A Narrative History of Combined Joint Task Force—Operation Inherent Resolve, 2015–2016*, n.d. [2016], 2, Hist Files, CMH.

136. Prepared Statement, Ashton B. Carter, 7 July 2015, *United States Strategy and Military Operations to Counter the Islamic State in Iraq and the Levant and United States Policy Toward Iraq and Syria*, 114 Cong. (21 May, 7 Jul, 16 Sep, 9 Dec 2015), 56, https://www.govinfo.gov/content/pkg/CHRG-114shrg21326/pdf/CHRG-114shrg21326.pdf, Hist Files, CMH. The cited statement was presented on 7 July 2015.

137. Lister, *Syrian Jihad*, 381–82; "U.S.-Trained Syrian Rebels Gave Equipment to Nusra: U.S. Military," Reuters, 26 Sep 2015, https://www.reuters.com/article/us-mideast-crisis-usa-equipment/u-s-trained-syrian-rebels-gave-equipment-to-nusra-u-s-military-idUSKCN0RP2HO20150926, Hist Files, CMH.

138. Michael D. Shear, Helene Cooper, and Eric Schmitt, "Obama Administration Ends Effort to Train Syrians to Combat ISIS," *New York Times*, 9 Oct 2015, https://www.nytimes.com/2015/10/10/world/middleeast/pentagon-program-islamic-state-syria.html, Hist Files, CMH; LIG-OCO, *Operation Inherent Resolve: September 30, 2015*, Rpt to Cong., 25 Nov 2015, 32.

139. Samuel Charap, Elina Treyger, and Edward Geist, *Understanding Russia's Intervention in Syria* (Santa Monica, CA: RAND Corporation, 2019), 11–12, https://www.rand.org/pubs/research_reports/RR3180.html, Hist Files, CMH.

140. Tim Ripley, *Operation Aleppo: Russia's War in Syria* (Lancaster, UK: Telic-Herrick Publications, 2018), 37.

141. DoD News Bfg, Col. Steven Warren, 4 Nov 2015, https://www.defense.gov/News/Transcripts/Transcript/Article/627718/

department-of-defense-press-briefing-by-colonel-warren-via-teleconference-from/, Hist Files, CMH.

142. Zachary Laub, "Syria's Civil War: The Descent Into Horror," Council on Foreign Relations, 17 May 2021, https://www.cfr.org/article/syrias-civil-war, Hist Files, CMH.

143. Carter, *A Lasting Defeat*, 36–38.

144. Carter, *A Lasting Defeat*, 19.

145. Gen. Raymond A. Thomas III, "SOCOM: Policing the World" (remarks, The Aspen Institute, 21 Jul 2017), 15–16, https://www.aspensecurityforum.org/asf-transcript-library, Hist Files, CMH; Shear, Cooper, and Schmitt, "Obama Administration Ends Effort to Train Syrians to Combat ISIS"; Ben Hubbard, "New U.S.-Backed Alliance to Counter ISIS in Syria Falters," *New York Times*, 2 Nov 2015, https://www.nytimes.com/2015/11/03/world/middleeast/new-us-backed-alliance-in-syria-exists-in-name-only.html, Hist Files, CMH.

146. DoD News Bfg, Warren, 13 Oct 2015.

147. DoD News Bfg, Senior Def Official, "Department of Defense Background Briefing on Enhancing Counter-ISIL Operations," 30 Oct 2015, https://www.defense.gov/News/Transcripts/Transcript/Article/626814/department-of-defense-background-briefing-on-enhancing-counter-isil-operations/, Hist Files, CMH.

148. Louise Shelley, "Blood Money: How ISIS Makes Bank," *Foreign Affairs*, 30 Nov 2014, https://www.foreignaffairs.com/articles/iraq/2014-11-30/blood-money, Hist Files, CMH; Michael R. Gordon and Eric Schmitt, "U.S. Steps Up Its Attacks on ISIS-Controlled Oil Fields in Syria," *New York Times*, 12 Nov 2015, https://www.nytimes.com/2015/11/13/us/politics/us-steps-up-its-attacks-on-isis-controlled-oil-fields-in-syria.html, Hist Files, CMH.

149. Wasser et al., *Air War Against the Islamic State*, 207, 217.

150. Wasser et al., *Air War Against the Islamic State*, 207–9; Gordon and Schmitt, "U.S. Steps Up Its Attacks on ISIS-Controlled Oil Fields in Syria"; LIG-OCO, *Operation Inherent Resolve: October 1, 2015–December 31, 2015*, 16 Feb 2016, 36.

151. Wasser et al., *Air War Against the Islamic State*, 206, 221–22.

152. Testimony, Ashton B. Carter, *Hearing to Receive Testimony on United States Military Strategy in the Middle East, Committee on Armed Services, United States Senate*, 114th Cong. (27 Oct 2015), 19, https://www.armed-services.senate.gov/imo/media/doc/15-81%20-%2010-27-15.pdf, Hist Files, CMH.

153. Gordon Lubold and Matt Bradley, "American Killed in Raid to Rescue Prisoners in Iraq," *Wall Street Journal*, 22 Oct 2015, https://www.wsj.com/amp/articles/american-killed-in-raid-to-rescue-kurdish-fighters-in-iraq-1445523452, Hist Files, CMH; Michael R. Gordon and Eric Schmitt, "U.S. Soldier Dies in

Raid to Free Prisoners of ISIS in Iraq," *New York Times*, 22 Oct 2015, https://www.nytimes.com/2015/10/23/world/middleeast/us-commandos-iraq-isis.html, Hist Files, CMH; "Thomas Patrick Payne," Congressional Medal of Honor Society, n.d., https://www.cmohs.org/recipients/thomas-p-payne, Hist Files, CMH.

154. Don Curren, "Canadian Soldier Killed, Three Others Wounded by Friendly Fire in Iraq," *Wall Street Journal*, 7 Mar 2015, https://www.wsj.com/amp/articles/canadian-soldier-killed-three-others-wounded-by-friendly-fire-in-iraq-1425758070, Hist Files, CMH.

155. Robert Burns, "Iraq's Stalemate in Ramadi Raises Doubts About U.S. Strategy," AP News, 26 Sep 2015, https://apnews.com/article/99ed293d3d1044bcafccef0aa6feb2c2, Hist Files, CMH; Patrick Martin, "Iraqi Security Forces Launch New Offensive in Ramadi," ISW, 8 Oct 2015, https://www.understandingwar.org/map/iraqi-security-forces-launch-new-offensive-ramadi, Hist Files, CMH.

156. DoD News Bfg, Warren, 13 Oct 2015; DoD News Bfg, Col. Steven Warren, 2 Dec 2015, https://www.defense.gov/News/Transcripts/Transcript/Article/632421/department-of-defense-press-briefing-by-col-warren-via-teleconference-from-bagh/, Hist Files, CMH.

157. Patrick Martin, "Ramadi Control Map, Dec. 9, 2015," ISW, 22 Dec 2015, https://www.understandingwar.org/map/ramadi-control-map-dec-9-2015, Hist Files, CMH.

158. Patrick Martin, "Iraq Situation Report: December 15–21, 2015," ISW, 21 Dec 2015, https://www.understandingwar.org/backgrounder/iraq-situation-report-december-15-21-2015, Hist Files, CMH.

159. DoD News Bfg, Col. Steven Warren, 22 Dec 2015, https://www.defense.gov/News/Transcripts/Transcript/Article/637800/department-of-defense-press-briefing-by-col-warren-via-teleconference-from-bagh/, Hist Files, CMH.

160. Falih Hassan, Sewell Chan, and Helene Cooper, "Celebrating Victory Over ISIS, Iraqi Leader Looks to Next Battles," *New York Times*, 29 Dec 2015, https://www.nytimes.com/2015/12/30/world/middleeast/haider-al-abadi-iraq-ramadi-isis.html, Hist Files, CMH.

161. According to the Iraqi Security Forces, around 500 Sunni tribal fighters deployed. See Jean Marc Mojon, "Sunni Tribal Fighters Deployed in Reconquered Ramadi Areas," Yahoo! News, 29 Dec 2015, https://www.yahoo.com/entertainment/sunni-tribal-fighters-deployed-reconquered-ramadi-areas-141209437.html, Hist Files, CMH. The full extent of the tribes' involvement in Ar Ramadi, however, is open to question. See Erin Cunningham, "Iraqi Forces Pushed ISIS from Ramadi. But Can the Shattered City Recover?," *Washington Post*, 16 Jan 2016, https://www.washingtonpost.com/world/middle_east/iraqi-forces-pushed-isis-from-ramadi-but-can-the-shattered-city-recover/2016/01/16/

def3569e-ba23-11e5-85cd-5ad59bc19432_story.html, Hist Files, CMH.

162. Andrew Tilghman, "'Squad-size' ISIS Units Remain in Ramadi," *Military Times*, 6 Jan 2016, https://www.militarytimes.com/2016/01/06/squad-size-isis-units-remain-in-ramadi/, Hist Files, CMH.

163. Hollie McKay, "Battle for Mosul Looms, as ISIS Digs in and Iraqis, Coalition Mass," Fox News, 22 Jan 2016, https://www.foxnews.com/world/battle-for-mosul-looms-as-isis-digs-in-and-iraqis-coalition-mass, Hist Files, CMH.

164. Michael R. Gordon, "Iraqi Forces and Shiite Militias Retake Oil Refinery From ISIS," *New York Times*, 16 Oct 2015, https://www.nytimes.com/2015/10/17/world/middleeast/iraqi-forces-and-shiite-militias-retake-oil-refinery-from-isis.html, Hist Files, CMH.

165. Rick Burns and Nickolas Zappone, *Threat Report: Iraq and Syria Update* (Fort Leavenworth, KS: TRADOC G-2 Analysis and Control Element Threats Integration, 2017), 15–16, https://community.apan.org/cfs-file/__key/docpreview-s/00-00-02-42-00/TR-Iraq_2D00_Syria-Update-AUG17.pdf, Hist Files, CMH; Patrick Martin, "Iraq Situation Report: November 10–19, 2015," ISW, 19 Nov 2015, https://www.understandingwar.org/backgrounder/iraq-situation-report-november-10-19-2015, Hist Files, CMH.

166. Aron Lund, "Taking the October Dam: Syria's Kurds Keep Hitting the Islamic State," *Diwan* (blog), Carnegie Endowment for International Peace, 28 Dec 2015, https://carnegie-mec.org/diwan/62363?lang=en/, Hist Files, CMH.

167. DoD News Bfg, Col. Steven Warren, 29 Dec 2015, https://www.defense.gov/News/Transcripts/Transcript/Article/639502/department-of-defense-press-briefing-by-colwarren-via-teleconference-from-baghd/, Hist Files, CMH.

168. Interv, Col. Christopher Eng, 7th Mil History Det (MHD), with Lt. Gen. Robert P. "Pat" White, CG, CJTF-OIR, 8 Sep 2020, 6, https://www.inherentresolve.mil/Releases/News-Releases/Article/2433175/transcript-of-oral-history-interview-ltg-r-pat-white-commander-cjtf-oir/, Hist Files, CMH.

169. Mark R. Reardon, "Reforging Babylon's Sword" (unpublished study, CMH, 2020), 779, Hist Files, CMH.

170. "82nd Airborne Division Transfers Command to 101st in Iraq," *Clarksville Now*, 8 Mar 2016, https://clarksvillenow.com/local/82nd-airborne-division-transfers-command-to-101st-in-iraq/, Hist Files, CMH.

171. DoD News Bfg, Col. Steven Warren, 21 Mar 2016, https://www.defense.gov/News/Transcripts/Transcript/Article/699172/department-of-defense-press-briefing-by-colonel-warren-via-teleconference-from/, Hist Files, CMH; Liz Sly and Mustafa Salim, "A U.S. Marine Is Killed in Iraq, the Second Combat Casualty of the ISIS War," *Washington Post*, 19 Mar 2016, https://www.washingtonpost.com/world/us-soldier-in-iraq-becomes-the-second-combat-death-in-war-against-islamic-state/2016/03/19/f906b677-4b5e-4840-a77c-64b19d7ef5e8_story.html,

Hist Files, CMH; Matthew L. Schehl, "Marines Identify Staff NCO Killed in ISIS Rocket Attack in Iraq," *Marine Corps Times*, 20 Mar 2016, https://www.marinecorpstimes.com/news/your-marine-corps/2016/03/20/marines-identify-staff-nco-killed-in-isis-rocket-attack-in-iraq/, Hist Files, CMH.

172. DoD News Bfg, Col. Steven Warren, 1 Apr 2016, https://www.defense.gov/News/Transcripts/Transcript/Article/711718/department-of-defense-press-briefing-by-colonel-warren-via-teleconference-from/, Hist Files, CMH.

173. LIG-OCO, *Operation Inherent Resolve: March 31, 2016*, Rpt to Cong., 6 May 2016, 30–31, https://www.dodig.mil/reports.html/Article/1159953/lead-inspector-general-for-operation-inherent-resolve-quarterly-report-to-the-u/, Hist Files, CMH.

174. Ryan Wylie, Aaron Childers, and Brett Sylvia, "Expeditionary Advising: Enabling Iraq Operations from the Gates of Baghdad through Eastern Mosul," *Small Wars Journal*, 22 Feb 2018, https://smallwarsjournal.com/jrnl/art/expeditionary-advising-enabling-iraqi-operations-gates-baghdad-through-eastern-mosul, Hist Files, CMH.

175. LIG-OCO, *Operation Inherent Resolve: March 31, 2016*, Rpt to Cong., 6 May 2016, 30–31; DoD News Bfg, Warren, 1 Apr 2016; "Iraq Halts ISIL Offensive as More Ground Troops Needed," Al Jazeera, 7 Apr 2016, https://www.aljazeera.com/news/2016/4/7/iraq-halts-isil-offensive-as-more-ground-troops-needed, Hist Files, CMH.

176. DoD News Bfg, Col. Steven Warren, 4 May 2016, https://www.defense.gov/Newsroom/Transcripts/Transcript/Article/751781/department-of-defense-press-briefing-by-col-warren-via-teleconference-from-bagh/, Hist Files, CMH.

177. LIG-OCO, *Operation Inherent Resolve: March 31, 2016*, 6 May 2016, 33.

178. "Security Forces Cut Off ISIS Supply Routes between Fallujah and Khalediya Island," *Iraqi News*, 2 Feb 2016, https://www.iraqinews.com/iraq-war/security-forces-cut-off-isis-supply-routes-fallujah-khalediya-island/, Hist Files, CMH.

179. LIG-OCO, *Operation Inherent Resolve: April 1, 2016–June 30, 2016*, Rpt to Cong., 5 Aug 2016, 35, https://www.dodig.mil/reports.html/Article/1150755/lead-inspector-general-for-operation-inherent-resolve-quarterly-report-to-the-u/, Hist Files, CMH; "Iraqi Forces 'Recapture IS-Held Town of Hit,'" BBC News, 14 Apr 2016, https://www.bbc.com/news/world-middle-east-36049780, Hist Files, CMH.

180. LIG-OCO, *Operation Inherent Resolve: April 1, 2016–June 30, 2016*, 5 Aug 2016, 35; Ghassan Adnan and Asa Fitch, "Iraqi Forces Recapture Strategic Town From Islamic State," *Wall Street Journal*, 19 May 2016, https://www.wsj.com/articles/iraqi-forces-recapture-strategic-town-from-islamic-state-1463662122,

Hist Files, CMH; Prepared Statement, Brett H. McGurk, *Global Efforts to Defeat ISIS: Hearing Before the Committee on Foreign Relations, United States Senate*, 114th Cong. (28 Jun 2016), 10, https://www.govinfo.gov/content/pkg/CHRG-114shrg28676/pdf/CHRG-114shrg28676.pdf, Hist Files, CMH.

181. "'Human Catastrophe' Unfolding Amid Battle for Fallujah," France24, 31 May 2016, https://www.france24.com/en/20160531-human-catastrophe-unfolding-civilians-fallujah-iraq-nrc-islamic-state, Hist Files, CMH.

182. Charlie d'Agata, "Battle Begins for City Where 100 American Troops Died," CBS News, 23 May 2016, https://www.cbsnews.com/news/iraq-isis-battle-fallujah-us-city-where-american-troops-killed-2004/, Hist Files, CMH.

183. Patrick Martin and ISW Iraq Team, "Iraq Situation Report: June 14–20, 2016," ISW, 20 Jun 2016, http://www.iswresearch.org/2016/06/iraq-situation-report-june-14-20-2016.html, Hist Files, CMH.

184. Jim Michaels, "Inside Look at U.S.-Led Coalition's Deadliest Single Attack on ISIL," *USA Today*, 12 Jul 2016, https://www.usatoday.com/story/news/world/2016/07/12/inside-look-us-led-coalitons-deadliest-single-attack-isil/86947394/, Hist Files, CMH. There are numerous conflicting accounts of this incident. Michaels's, written almost two weeks after the fact, is perhaps the best and most detailed. In his blog, *Musings on Iraq*, Joel Wing gives a comprehensive breakdown of the different version of what exactly happened to the ISIS convoy (and when). See Joel Wing, "Islamic State's Highway of Death in Iraq's Anbar," *Musings on Iraq*, 17 Jul 2016, http://musingsoniraq.blogspot.com/2016/07/islamic-states-highway-of-death-in.html, Hist Files, CMH.

185. See, for example, Mustafa Salim and Thomas Gibbons-Neff, "Iraqi, U.S. Aircraft Bomb Convoy of Islamic State Fighters Fleeing Fallujah With Their Families," *Washington Post*, 30 Jun 2016, https://www.washingtonpost.com/news/checkpoint/wp/2016/06/30/iraqi-gunships-u-s-jets-target-islamic-state-convoys-outside-fallujah-and-ramadi/, Hist Files, CMH.

186. LIG-OCO, *Operation Inherent Resolve: April 1, 2016–June 30, 2016*, 5 Aug 2016, 36; *Iraq: Turning a Blind Eye: The Arming of the Popular Mobilization Units* (London: Amnesty International, 2017), 18, https://www.amnestyusa.org/files/iraq_report_turning_a_blind_eye.pdf, Hist Files, CMH. See also Lawk Ghafuri, "Fallujah: Hundreds of Sunnis Missing 3 Years After PMF Retook City," Rudaw, 29 Sep 2019, https://www.rudaw.net/english/middleeast/iraq/29092019, Hist Files, CMH.

187. Falih Hassan, Tim Arango, and Omar Al-Jawoshy, "Bombing Kills More than 140 in Baghdad," *New York Times*, 3 Jul 2016, https://www.nytimes.com/2016/07/04/world/middleeast/baghdad-bombings.html, Hist Files, CMH; Ahmed Rasheed, "Baghdad Bombing Death Toll Rises to 292: health ministry," Reuters, 7 Jul 2016, https://www.reuters.com/article/idCAKCN0ZN1AD, Hist

Files, CMH.

188. Karen Yourish et al., "Where ISIS Has Directed and Inspired Attacks Around the World," *New York Times*, 16 Jul 2016, https://www.nytimes.com/interactive/2015/06/17/world/middleeast/map-isis-attacks-around-the-world.html, Hist Files, CMH.

189. LIG-OCO, *Operation Inherent Resolve: March 31, 2016*, 6 May 2016, 33.

190. Kogon, *Sky Dragon Dismantles the "Caliphate,"* 13; Philip Issa, "Syrian Rebels Take Border Crossing from IS," *Washington Post*, 5 Mar 2016, https://www.washingtonpost.com/world/syria-rebels-battle-islamic-state-for-control-of-iraq-crossing/2016/03/05/e481d274-e319-11e5-9c36-e1902f6b6571_story.html, Hist Files, CMH.

191. Darlene Superville, "250 U.S. Troops Are Deploying to Syria as ISIS Fight Intensifies," *Military Times*, 24 Apr 2016, https://www.militarytimes.com/flashpoints/2016/04/25/250-u-s-troops-are-deploying-to-syria-as-isis-fight-intensifies/, Hist Files, CMH.

192. LIG-OCO, *Operation Inherent Resolve: April 1, 2016–June 30, 2016*, 5 Aug 2016, 39-41; LIG-OCO, *Operation Inherent Resolve: July 1, 2016–September 30, 2016*, Rpt to Cong., 4 Nov 2016, 41–42, https://www.dodig.mil/reports.html/Article/1150745/lead-inspector-general-for-operation-inherent-resolve-quarterly-report-to-the-u/, Hist Files, CMH.

193. Memo, Lt. Col. David R. Waters, Dep Cdr, 2d Inf Bde Combat Team (IBCT), for Col. Brett Sylvia, Cdr, 2d IBCT–Task Force Strike, 10 Apr 2017, sub: Task Force Strike Operation Inherent Resolve (OIR) History, 5, Hist Files, CMH; Emily Anagnostos, "Iraq Situation Report: July 7–13, 2016," ISW, 13 Jul 2016, https://www.understandingwar.org/backgrounder/iraq-situation-report-july-7-13-2016, Hist Files, CMH; Dan Lamothe and Loveday Morris, "Pentagon Will Send Hundreds More Troops to Iraq Following Seizure of Key Airfield," *Washington Post*, 11 Jul 2016, https://www.washingtonpost.com/news/checkpoint/wp/2016/07/11/seizure-of-key-air-base-near-mosul-raises-prospect-of-u-s-escalation-against-isis/, Hist Files, CMH.

194. Memo, Waters for Sylvia, 10 Apr 2017, sub: Task Force Strike OIR History, 3, 6.

195. Robert Sisk, "101st Soldiers Deploying to Bolster Fight Against ISIS in Iraq," Military.com, 8 Aug 2016, https://www.military.com/daily-news/2016/08/08/101st-soldiers-deploying-to-bolster-fight-against-isis-in-iraq.html, Hist Files, CMH.

196. "'Strike' Brigade Command Team Set to Return from Iraq Wednesday, Uncase Colors," *Clarksville Now*, 23 Jan 2017, https://clarksvillenow.com/local/strike-brigade-command-team-set-to-return-from-iraq-wednesday-uncase-

colors/, Hist Files, CMH.

197. CJTF-OIR Press Release, "CJTF-OIR Transitions Commanders in the Mission to Destroy Da'esh," 22 Aug 2016, https://www.inherentresolve.mil/Releases/News-Releases/Article/921016/cjtf-oir-transitions-commanders-in-the-mission-to-destroy-daesh/, Hist Files, CMH.

198. Bfg, Lt. Gen. Sean B. MacFarland to U.S. Army Maneuver Center of Excellence (MCoE) Conf, 20 Sep 2016, sub: Hybrid Maneuver, slides 8, 10, 26, Hist Files, CMH.

199. LIG-OCO, *Operation Inherent Resolve: July 1, 2016–September 30, 2016*, 4 Nov 2016, 39.

200. Memo, Waters for Sylvia, 10 Apr 2017, sub: Task Force Strike OIR History, 6–7.

201. LIG-OCO, *Operation Inherent Resolve: July 1, 2016 – September 30, 2016*, 4 Nov 2016, 28, 32.

202. Kogon, *Sky Dragon Dismantles the "Caliphate,"* 15.

203. Kogon, *Sky Dragon Dismantles the "Caliphate,"* 14–15.

204. Kogon, *Sky Dragon Dismantles the "Caliphate,"* 24–25; Campbell MacDiarmid, "Mosul University after ISIL: Damaged but Defiant," Al Jazeera, 26 Jan 2017, https://www.aljazeera.com/features/2017/1/26/mosul-university-after-isil-damaged-but-defiant, Hist Files, CMH.

205. Kogon, *Sky Dragon Dismantles the "Caliphate,"* 15.

206. Kogon, *Sky Dragon Dismantles the "Caliphate,"* 15–17.

207. Press Conf, Barack H. Obama and Matteo Renzi, 18 Oct 2016, https://obamawhitehouse.archives.gov/the-press-office/2016/10/18/press-conference-president-obama-and-prime-minister-renzi-republic-italy, Hist Files, CMH.

208. Kogon, *Sky Dragon Dismantles the "Caliphate,"* 18–19.

209. Mosul Study Gp, "What the Battle for Mosul Teaches the Force," No. 17-24 (Fort Leavenworth, KS: U.S. Army Combined Arms Center, 2017), 7, Hist Files, CMH.

210. Kogon, *Sky Dragon Dismantles the "Caliphate,"* 20–21; "Iraqi Forces Drive ISIS from Tal Afar Airbase," Al Arabiya, 16 Nov 2016, https://english.alarabiya.net/News/middle-east/2016/11/16/Iraqi-units-ready-to-storm-airbase-west-of-Mosul-, Hist Files, CMH; LIG-OCO, *Operation Inherent Resolve: October 1, 2016–December 31, 2016*, Rpt to Cong., 2 Feb 2017, 33, https://www.dodig.mil/reports.html/Article/1150728/lead-inspector-general-for-operation-inherent-resolve-quarterly-report-to-the-u/, Hist Files, CMH.

211. Kogon, *Sky Dragon Dismantles the "Caliphate,"* 21.

212. Kogon, *Sky Dragon Dismantles the "Caliphate,"* 22.

213. Kogon, *Sky Dragon Dismantles the "Caliphate,"* 22–23; Emily Anagnostos, "The Campaign for Mosul: December 6–12, 2016," ISW, 12

Dec 2016, http://www.understandingwar.org/backgrounder/campaign-mosul-december-6-12-2016, Hist Files, CMH; Susannah George, "A Lethal Mistake Leads to a Harrowing Ambush in Iraq's Mosul," AP News, 8 Dec 2016, https://apnews.com/d6f0788b20b341788d2135c9e4060575, Hist Files, CMH.

214. Anagnostos, "Campaign for Mosul: December 6–12, 2016."

215. Kogon, *Sky Dragon Dismantles the "Caliphate,"* 23.

216. Kogon, *Sky Dragon Dismantles the "Caliphate,"* 20; U.S. Army Press Release, "Department of the Army Announces 1st Infantry Division Deployment," 19 Oct 2016, https://www.army.mil/article/176761/department_of_the_army_announces_1st_infantry_division_deployment, Hist Files, CMH.

217. CENTCOM Press Release #20170119-02, "Air Assault, All American Brigades Complete Transfer of Authority in Iraq," 19 Jan 2017, https://www.centcom.mil/MEDIA/PRESS-RELEASES/Press-Release-View/Article/1054168/air-assault-all-american-brigades-complete-transfer-of-authority-in-iraq/, Hist Files, CMH.

218. Kogon, *Sky Dragon Dismantles the "Caliphate,"* 24.

219. Stephen Kalin and Ahmed Rasheed, "Iraqi Forces Reach Tigris in Mosul as Suicide Bombs Hit Baghdad," Reuters, 8 Jan 2017, https://www.reuters.com/article/us-mideast-crisis-iraq-mosul/iraqi-forces-reach-tigris-in-mosul-as-suicide-bombs-hit-baghdad-idUSKBN14S0LP, Hist Files, CMH.

220. Emily Anagnostos, "The Campaign for Mosul: January 10–18, 2017," ISW, 18 Jan 2017, http://www.understandingwar.org/backgrounder/campaign-mosul-january-10-18-2017, Hist Files, CMH.

221. Kogon, *Sky Dragon Dismantles the "Caliphate,"* 25; "Haidar al-Abadi: East Mosul Fully Liberated from ISIL," Al Jazeera, 24 Jan 2017, https://www.aljazeera.com/news/2017/1/24/haider-al-abadi-east-mosul-fully-liberated-from-isil, Hist Files, CMH.

222. DoD News Bfg, Sec Def James N. Mattis, CJCS Gen. Joseph F. Dunford, Jr., and Special Envoy Brett H. McGurk, 19 May 2017, https://www.defense.gov/Newsroom/Transcripts/Transcript/Article/1188225/department-of-defense-press-briefing-by-secretary-mattis-general-dunford-and-sp/, Hist Files, CMH; Martin Pengelly, "Defense Secretary Mattis Says US Policy Against Isis Is Now 'Annihilation'," *Guardian,* 28 May 2017, https://www.theguardian.com/us-news/2017/may/28/james-mattis-defense-secretary-us-isis-annihilation, Hist Files, CMH.

223. Kogon, *Sky Dragon Dismantles the "Caliphate,"* 25–27.

224. Emily Anagnostos, "The Campaign for Mosul: February 1–21, 2017," ISW, 21 Feb 2017, http://www.understandingwar.org/backgrounder/campaign-mosul-february-1-21-2017, Hist Files, CMH.

225. Emily Anagnostos and ISW Iraq Team, "The Campaign for Mosul:

February 22–24, 2017," ISW, 24 Feb 2017, http://www.understandingwar.org/backgrounder/campaign-mosul-february-22-24-2017, Hist Files, CMH.

226. Mosul Study Gp, "What the Battle for Mosul Teaches the Force," 82; Interv, Michael Lynch, U.S. Army Heritage and Education Center, with Col. James P. Work, Cdr, 2d Bde Combat Team (BCT), 82d Abn Div, 7 May 2017, 5, Hist Files, CMH; Kogon, *Sky Dragon Dismantles the "Caliphate,"* 26.

227. Emily Anagnostos, "The Campaign for Mosul: February 22–March 1, 2017," ISW, 1 Mar 2017, http://www.understandingwar.org/backgrounder/campaign-mosul-february-22-march-1-2017, Hist Files, CMH; Kogon, *Sky Dragon Dismantles the "Caliphate,"* 27.

228. AAR, Opn EAGLE STRIKE, Task Force CHARGER, 1st Bn, 12th Cav, 22 Feb–26 Jul 2017, 18 Jan 2018, 5–6, Hist Files, CMH; Emily Anagnostos, "The Campaign for Mosul, March 9–16, 2017," ISW, 16 Mar 2017, http://www.understandingwar.org/backgrounder/campaign-mosul-march-9-16-2017, Hist Files, CMH.

229. Kogon, *Sky Dragon Dismantles the "Caliphate,"* 28–30.

230. Jessa Rose Dury-Agri, Patrick Martin, and ISW Iraq Team, "The Campaign for Mosul: March 2–April 28," ISW, 28 Apr 2017, http://www.understandingwar.org/backgrounder/campaign-mosul-march-2-april-28, Hist Files, CMH. Casualty figures for different phases of the battle can be found in Kogon, *Sky Dragon Dismantles the "Caliphate,"* 34.

231. Kogon, *Sky Dragon Dismantles the "Caliphate,"* 31.

232. Kogon, *Sky Dragon Dismantles the "Caliphate,"* 32; "Iraqi Forces Repel Islamic State Counter-Attack in West Mosul – Police," Reuters, 14 Jun 2017, https://www.reuters.com/article/us-mideast-crisis-iraq-mosul/iraqi-forces-repel-islamic-state-counter-attack-in-west-mosul-police-idUSKBN1951HE, Hist Files, CMH.

233. Kogon, *Sky Dragon Dismantles the "Caliphate,"* 32–34.

234. "Chief Petty Officer Jason C. Finan," *Military Times*, n.d., https://the-fallen.militarytimes.com/chief-petty-officer-jason-c-finan/6568689, Hist Files, CMH.

235. "1st Lt. Weston C. Lee," *Military Times*, n.d., https://thefallen.militarytimes.com/1st-lt-weston-c-lee/6568703, Hist Files, CMH; Greg Toppo, "IED Near Mosul Kills U.S. Army Platoon Leader," *USA Today*, 30 Apr 2017, https://www.usatoday.com/story/news/2017/04/30/mosul-iraq-platoon-leader-killed/101142188/, Hist Files, CMH.

236. Interv, Col. Jason Awadi, Lt. Col. James Gill, and Donald Haus, CALL, with Maj. Gen. Joseph M. Martin, CG, 1st Inf Div and CJFLCC-OIR, 26 Oct 2017, 3–4, Hist Files, CMH.

237. Kogon, *Sky Dragon Dismantles the "Caliphate,"* 32.

238. Interv, Awadi, Gill, and Haus, with Martin, 26 Oct 2017, 4–5.

239. AAR, Opn EAGLE STRIKE, Task Force CHARGER, 1st Bn, 12th Cav, 18 Jan 2018, 5.

240. Interv, Awadi, Gill, and Haus, with Martin, 26 Oct 2017, 8.

241. Kogon, *Sky Dragon Dismantles the "Caliphate,"* 37.

242. Raqqah Study Gp, "What the Battle for Raqqah Teaches the Force," Asymmetric Warfare Gp No. 18-13 (Fort Meade, MD: Asymmetric Warfare Group, 2018), 5, 7, 33.

243. Kogon, *Sky Dragon Dismantles the "Caliphate,"* 41; "City Walls of Rafiqa (Raqqa) and the Baghdad Gate," Museum with No Frontiers, n.d., https://islamicart.museumwnf.org/database_item.php?id=monument;ISL;sy;Mon01;29;en, Hist Files, CMH.

244. LIG-OCO, *Operation Inherent Resolve: October 1, 2016–December 31, 2016*, 2 Feb 2017, 35–37.

245. LIG-OCO, *Operation Inherent Resolve: October 1, 2016–December 31, 2016*, 2 Feb 2017, 26.

246. Raqqah Study Gp, "What the Battle for Raqqah Teaches the Force," 21–22; "Kurdish People's Protection Unit YPG," GlobalSecurity.org, n.d., https://www.globalsecurity.org/military/world/para/ypg.htm, Hist Files, CMH.

247. Raqqah Study Gp, "What the Battle for Raqqah Teaches the Force," 3, 22; John Ismay, "U.S. Says 2,000 Troops Are in Syria, a Fourfold Increase," *New York Times*, 6 Dec 2017, https://www.nytimes.com/2017/12/06/world/middleeast/us-troops-syria.html, Hist Files, CMH.

248. Raqqah Study Gp, "What the Battle for Raqqah Teaches the Force," 6.

249. Wasser et al., *Air War Against the Islamic State*, 190–91.

250. Genevieve Casagrande, "The Campaign for Ar-Raqqah: January 12, 2017," ISW, 12 Jan 2017, http://www.understandingwar.org/backgrounder/campaign-ar-raqqah-january-12-2017, Hist Files, CMH.

251. LIG-OCO, *Operation Inherent Resolve: October 1, 2016–December 31, 2016*, 2 Feb 2017, 36–37.

252. Casagrande, "Campaign for Ar-Raqqah: January 12, 2017."

253. Kogon, *Sky Dragon Dismantles the "Caliphate,"* 39.

254. Chris Kozak, "Syria Situation Report: March 2–9, 2017," ISW, 9 Mar 2017, http://www.understandingwar.org/backgrounder/syria-situation-report-march-2-9-2017, Hist Files, CMH.

255. Kogon, *Sky Dragon Dismantles the "Caliphate,"* 38–39.

256. Tom Ramage, "The Campaign for Ar-Raqqah, February 24, 2017," ISW, 24 Feb 2017, http://www.understandingwar.org/backgrounder/campaign-ar-raqqah-february-24-2017, Hist Files, CMH.

257. Kogon, *Sky Dragon Dismantles the "Caliphate,"* 39–40; Chris Kozak,

"Syria Situation Report: March 17–30, 2017," ISW, 30 Mar 2017, http://www.understandingwar.org/backgrounder/syria-situation-report-march-17-30-2017, Hist Files, CMH.

258. Michael R. Gordon and Eric Schmitt, "Trump to Arm Syrian Kurds, Even as Turkey Strongly Objects," *New York Times*, 9 May 2017, https://www.nytimes.com/2017/05/09/us/politics/trump-kurds-syria-army.html, Hist Files, CMH.

259. Kogon, *Sky Dragon Dismantles the "Caliphate,"* 40–41.

260. Raqqah Study Gp, "What the Battle for Raqqah Teaches the Force," 7.

261. Lisa Barrington, "U.S.-Backed Forces Seize Raqqa Ruins; U.N. Sees 'Dire' Situation," Reuters, 7 Jun 2017, https://www.reuters.com/article/us-mideast-crisis-syria-raqqa/u-s-backed-forces-seize-raqqa-ruins-u-n-sees-dire-situation-idUSKBN18Y34H, Hist Files, CMH.

262. Kogon, *Sky Dragon Dismantles the "Caliphate,"* 41.

263. Hassan Hassan, "The Battle for Raqqa and the Challenges after Liberation," *CTC Sentinel* 10, no. 6 (Jun/Jul 2017): 5.

264. Kogon, *Sky Dragon Dismantles the "Caliphate,"* 41; CJTF-OIR Press Release, "SDF Breaches Old City of Raqqah," 4 Jul 2017, https://www.inherentresolve.mil/Releases/News-Releases/Article/1236853/sdf-breaches-old-city-of-raqqah/, Hist Files, CMH.

265. Kogon, *Sky Dragon Dismantles the "Caliphate,"* 42; Raqqah Study Gp, "What the Battle for Raqqah Teaches the Force," 9.

266. "Funk Journal" (unpublished, Army University Press, Fort Leavenworth, KS, 2020), 21, Hist Files, CMH.

267. Raqqah Study Gp, "What the Battle for Raqqah Teaches the Force," 9.

268. Raqqah Study Gp, "What the Battle for Raqqah Teaches the Force," 9.

269. Christopher Mele, "Scott Dayton Identified as First American to Die in Syria Combat," *New York Times*, 25 Nov 2016, https://www.nytimes.com/2016/11/25/world/middleeast/scott-dayton-died-syria-sailor-killed.html, Hist Files, CMH.

270. Ministère des Armées Press Release, "Hommages à l'adjudant-chef Stéphane Grenier, sous-officier du 13e RDP mort pour la France" [Tributes to Chief Warrant Officer Stéphane Grenier, noncommissioned officer of the 13th RDP who died for France], 30 Sep 2017, https://www.defense.gouv.fr/terre/actu-terre/hommages-a-l-adjudant-chef-stephane-grenier-sous-officier-du-13e-rdp-mort-pour-la-france, Hist Files, CMH.

271. Raqqah Study Gp, "What the Battle for Raqqah Teaches the Force," 9.

272. Luke Mogelson, "Dark Victory in Raqqa," *New Yorker*, 30 Oct 2017, https://www.newyorker.com/magazine/2017/11/06/dark-victory-in-raqqa, Hist Files, CMH.

273. Kogon, *Sky Dragon Dismantles the "Caliphate,"* 42–43.

274. Kogon, *Sky Dragon Dismantles the "Caliphate,"* 44.

275. CJTF-OIR Press Release, Sgt. Von Marie Donato, "1st Infantry Division Transfers Mission to 1st Armored Division," 12 Jul 2017, https://www.dvidshub.net/news/240879/1st-infantry-division-transfers-mission-1st-armored-division, Hist Files, CMH.

276. Kogon, *Sky Dragon Dismantles the "Caliphate,"* 35.

277. Interv, CALL and 20th MHD, with Lt. Gen. Paul E. Funk II, CG, CJTF-OIR, 27 Jan 2018, 2–3, Hist Files, CMH.

278. Kogon, *Sky Dragon Dismantles the "Caliphate,"* 35.

279. Alex Lockie, "ISIS Fighters, Once Bent on Martyrdom, Surrender en Masse from Last Iraqi Stronghold," *Business Insider*, 9 Oct 2017, https://www.businessinsider.com/isis-fighters-surrender-en-mass-iraq-2017-10, Hist Files, CMH; CJTF-OIR Press Release, "Iraqi Security Forces Liberate Hawijah," 5 Oct 2017, https://www.inherentresolve.mil/Releases/News-Releases/Article/1334857/iraqi-security-forces-liberate-hawijah/, Hist Files, CMH.

280. CJTF-OIR Press Release, "Iraqi Security Forces Liberate Al Qaim," 4 Nov 2017, https://www.inherentresolve.mil/Releases/News-Releases/Article/1363100/iraqi-security-forces-liberate-al-qaim/, Hist Files, CMH.

281. Margaret Coker and Falih Hassan, "Iraq Prime Minister Declares Victory Over ISIS," *New York Times*, 9 Dec 2017, https://www.nytimes.com/2017/12/09/world/middleeast/iraq-isis-haider-al-abadi.html, Hist Files, CMH.

282. Song Lifang, "Over 2,000 IS Militants Killed in Iraq's Tal Afar," Xinhua, 3 Sep 2017, http://www.xinhuanet.com//english/2017-09/03/c_136577714.htm (page discontinued), Hist Files, CMH.

283. Michelle Tan, "Pentagon Identifies Two Soldiers Killed in Artillery Incident in Iraq," *Army Times*, 14 Aug 2017, https://www.armytimes.com/news/your-army/2017/08/15/pentagon-identifies-two-soldiers-killed-in-artillery-incident-in-iraq/, Hist Files, CMH; Corey Dickstein, "82nd Airborne Soldiers Killed in Iraq Artillery Mishap Were from Texas, New York City," *Stars and Stripes*, 15 Aug 2017, https://www.stripes.com/news/army/82nd-airborne-soldiers-killed-in-iraq-artillery-mishap-were-from-texas-new-york-city-1.482968, Hist Files, CMH.

284. Corey Dickstein, "Soldier Killed in Iraq Bomb Blast Was Just Starting First Deployment," *Stars and Stripes*, 3 Oct 2017, https://www.stripes.com/news/soldier-killed-in-iraq-bomb-blast-was-just-starting-first-deployment-1.490738, Hist Files, CMH; Devon L. Suits, "American Soldiers, Partners Enriched by 10th Mountain OIR Rotation," U.S. Army News Service, 7 Aug 2018, https://www.army.mil/article/209366/american_soldiers_partners_enriched_by_10th_mountain_oir_rotation, Hist Files, CMH.

285. LIG-OCO, *Operation Inherent Resolve and Operation Pacific*

Eagle–Philippines: January 1, 2018–March 31, 2018, Rpt to Cong., 4 May 2018, 14–15, https://www.dodig.mil/reports.html/Article/1512438/lead-inspector-general-for-operation-inherent-resolve-and-operation-pacific-eag/, Hist Files, CMH.

286. LIG-OCO, *Operation Inherent Resolve and Operation Pacific Eagle–Philippines: April 1, 2018–June 30, 2018*, Rpt to Cong., 6 Aug 2018, 18–19, https://www.dodig.mil/reports.html/Article/1594251/lead-inspector-general-for-operation-inherent-resolve-and-operation-pacific-eag/, Hist Files, CMH.

287. CJTF-OIR Press Release, "Combined Joint Forces Land Component Command Deactivation Ceremony," 30 Apr 2018, https://www.inherentresolve.mil/Releases/News-Releases/Article/1506377/combined-joint-forces-land-component-command-deactivation-ceremony/, Hist Files, CMH.

288. LIG-OCO, *Operation Inherent Resolve and Operation Pacific Eagle–Philippines: July 1, 2018–September 30, 2018*, Rpt to Cong., 5 Nov 2018, 3, https://www.dodig.mil/reports.html/Article/1681560/lead-inspector-general-for-operation-inherent-resolve-i-quarterly-report-to-the/, Hist Files, CMH.

289. "Iraq's Civilian Death Toll Drops by Nearly 80 Percent: Reports," Rudaw, 10 Jun 2018, https://www.rudaw.net/english/middleeast/iraq/090620183, Hist Files, CMH. According to preliminary data collected by Iraq Body Count, 2018 saw the lowest number of civilian deaths in Iraq since the beginning of Operation Iraqi Freedom in 2003. See Iraq Body Count Database, n.d., https://www.iraqbodycount.org/database/ (accessed 3 Jan 2022).

290. "Iraqis Vote in First Election Since ISIL Defeat; UN Chief Hails Polls as Progress on Path to Stronger Democracy," UN News, 13 May 2018, https://news.un.org/en/story/2018/05/1009592, Hist Files, CMH.

291. LIG-OCO, *Operation Inherent Resolve and Operation Pacific Eagle–Philippines: October 1, 2017–December 31, 2017*, Rpt to Cong., 2 Feb 2018, 19, https://www.dodig.mil/reports.html/Article/1430685/lead-inspector-general-for-operation-inherent-resolve-and-operation-pacific-eag/, Hist Files, CMH.

292. LIG-OCO, *Operation Inherent Resolve and Operation Pacific Eagle–Philippines: April 1, 2018–June 30, 2018*, 6 Aug 2018, 3, 19–20.

293. "Syrian Army, Allies Reach Airbase Besieged by Islamic State In Eastern Syria: Commander," Reuters, 9 Sep 2017, https://www.reuters.com/article/us-mideast-crisis-syria/syrian-army-allies-reach-airbase-besieged-by-islamic-state-in-eastern-syria-commander-idUSKCN1BK0IL?il=0, Hist Files, CMH; "Syria Declares Victory Over Islamic State in Deir al-Zor," Reuters, 3 Nov 2017, https://www.reuters.com/article/us-mideast-crisis-syria-deiralzor/syria-declares-victory-over-islamic-state-in-deir-al-zor-idUSKBN1D30IE, Hist Files, CMH.

294. LIG-OCO, *Operation Inherent Resolve and Operation Pacific Eagle–Philippines: October 1, 2017–December 31, 2017*, 2 Feb 2018, 5, 25, 27–28, 33;

Tom Perry and Lisa Barrington, "U.S.-Backed Campaign Against IS in Eastern Syria to Speed Up: SDF Militia," Yahoo! News, 18 Oct 20017, https://news.yahoo.com/u-backed-campaign-against-eastern-syria-speed-sdf-103428630.html, Hist Files, CMH; Michal Kranz, "This Map Shows How ISIS Has Been Almost Completely Wiped Out," *Business Insider*, 22 Dec 2017, https://www.businessinsider.com/map-of-isis-territory-2017-12, Hist Files, CMH.

295. Thomas Gibbons-Neff, "How a 4-hour Battle Between Russian Mercenaries and U.S. Commandos Unfolded in Syria," *New York Times*, 24 May 2018, https://www.nytimes.com/2018/05/24/world/middleeast/american-commandos-russian-mercenaries-syria.html, Hist Files, CMH.

296. "Syria War: Thousands Flee Turkish Assault on Afrin Enclave," BBC News, 23 Jan 2018, https://www.bbc.com/news/world-middle-east-42788054, Hist Files, CMH.

297. LIG-OCO, *Operation Inherent Resolve and Operation Pacific Eagle–Philippines: January 1, 2018–March 31, 2018*, 4 May 2018, 24–25.

298. Zeynep Bilginsoy and Sarah El Deeb, "Turkey-Backed Forces Capture Syrian Kurdish Town of Afrin," AP News, 18 Mar 2018, https://apnews.com/53578ec31e9748fba19f2f33f0e25224/Turkey-backed-forces-capture-Syrian-Kurdish-town-of-Afrin, Hist Files, CMH.

299. William Gallo, "Mattis: Turkish Offensive 'Distracts' from Anti-IS Fight," Voice of America News, 23 Jan 2018, https://www.voanews.com/usa/mattis-turkish-offensive-distracts-anti-fight, Hist Files, CMH.

300. Hassan Hassan, "A Hollow Victory Over the Islamic State in Syria? The High Risk of Jihadi Revival in Deir ez-Zor's Euphrates River Valley," *CTC Sentinel* 12, no. 2 (Feb 2019): 2.

301. Rob Alsworth and Andrew Tidmarsh, "Lessons for Military Planning in 21st Century Warfare: Shaping the Military Defeat of Daesh in the Middle Euphrates River Valley," *RUSI Journal* 163, no. 5 (Oct/Nov 2018): 56.

302. Chad Garland, "2018 Blast in Syria That Killed US, UK soldiers Accidental Detonation, Not Enemy Action," *Stars and Stripes*, 29 Jul 2019, https://www.stripes.com/news/middle-east/2018-blast-in-syria-that-killed-us-uk-soldiers-accidental-detonation-not-enemy-action-1.592406 (page discontinued), Hist Files, CMH.

303. Barbara Starr, "US and British Soldiers Killed in Syria Were on ISIS 'Kill or Capture' Mission," CNN, 2 Apr 2018, https://www.cnn.com/2018/04/02/politics/us-british-soldiers-killed-syria-isis-kill-mission/index.html, Hist Files, CMH.

304. Joseph Trevithick, "How a Secretive Special Operations Task Force is Taking the Fight to ISIS," *The War Zone*, 1 May 2017, https://www.thedrive.com/the-war-zone/9848/how-a-secretive-special-operations-task-force-is-taking-the-fight-to-isis, Hist Files, CMH.

305. CJTF-OIR Press Release, "Coalition Forces, Partners Initiate Second Phase of Operation Roundup," 3 Jun 2018, https://www.inherentresolve.mil/Releases/News-Releases/Article/1538866/coalition-forces-partners-initiate-second-phase-of-operation-roundup/, Hist Files, CMH.

306. CJTF-OIR Press Release, "Ground Offensive Begins for Operation Roundup, Phase Three," 11 Sep 2018, https://www.inherentresolve.mil/Releases/News-Releases/Article/1626665/ground-offensive-begins-for-operation-round-up-phase-three/, Hist Files, CMH.

307. Alexandra N. Gutowski and Sarah Nadler, "US Has Launched Over 500 Strikes Against the Islamic State Since May," *FDD's Long War Journal*, 3 Aug 2018, https://www.longwarjournal.org/archives/2018/08/roundup.php, Hist Files, CMH.

308. CJTF-OIR Press Release, "Ground Offensive Begins for Operation Roundup, Phase Three," 11 Sep 2018.

309. CJTF-OIR Press Release, "Operation Inherent Resolve Transitions Commanders for Defeat-ISIS Mission," 13 Sep 2018, http://www.inherentresolve.mil:80/News/News-Releases/Article/1631032/cjtf-oir-transitions-commanders-for-defeat-isis-mission/ (page discontinued), Hist Files, CMH.

310. "Hajin, One of the Last Towns Held by IS Militants Falls in Syria," Deutsche Welle, 14 Dec 2018, https://www.dw.com/en/hajin-one-of-the-last-towns-held-by-is-militants-falls-in-syria/a-46737216, Hist Files, CMH.

311. Falih Hassan and Rod Nordland, "Battered ISIS Keeps Grip on Last Piece of Territory for Over a Year," *New York Times*, 9 Dec 2018, https://www.nytimes.com/2018/12/09/world/middleeast/isis-territory-syria-iraq.html, Hist Files, CMH.

312. Wasser et al., *Air War Against the Islamic State*, 406; Rukmini Callimachi, "ISIS Caliphate Crumbles as Last Village in Syria Falls," *New York Times*, 23 Mar 2019, https://www.nytimes.com/2019/03/23/world/middleeast/isis-syria-caliphate.html, Hist Files, CMH.

313. "Hajin, One Of The Last Towns Held by IS Militants Falls in Syria."

314. Callimachi, "ISIS Caliphate Crumbles as Last Village in Syria Falls."

315. William Branigin, Katie Mettler, and Missy Ryan, "Americans Slain in Syria Attack: A Green Beret, a Former SEAL and Two Language Specialists," *Washington Post*, 18 Jan 2019, https://www.washingtonpost.com/world/national-security/pentagon-identifies-three-of-the-four-americans-killed-in-syria-suicide-bombing/2019/01/18/5c9f31b8-1b1e-11e9-88fe-f9f77a3bcb6c_story.html, Hist Files, CMH.

316. U.S. Embassy in Syria Press Release, "Statement of the President on the Liberation of ISIS-Controlled Territory," 23 Mar 2019, https://sy.usembassy.gov/statement-from-the-president-on-the-liberation-of-isis-controlled-territory/, Hist

Files, CMH.

317. LIG-OCO, *Operation Inherent Resolve: April 1, 2019–June 30, 2019*, Rpt to Cong., 2 Aug 2019, 16–17, https://www.dodig.mil/reports. html/Article/1926689/lead-inspector-general-for-operation-inherent-resolve-quarterly-report-to-the-u/, Hist Files, CMH.

318. "US Troops Start Pullout in Syria as Turkey Prepares Operation," Al Jazeera, 7 Oct 2019, https://www.aljazeera.com/news/2019/10/7/us-troops-start-pullout-in-syria-as-turkey-prepares-operation, Hist Files, CMH; CENTCOM Press Release #20190914-01, "CJTF-OIR Transitions Commanders for Defeat-ISIS Mission," 14 Sep 2019, https://www.centcom.mil/MEDIA/PRESS-RELEASES/Press-Release-View/Article/1960770/cjtf-oir-transitions-commanders-for-defeat-isis-mission/, Hist Files, CMH.

319. LIG-OCO, *Operation Inherent Resolve: July 1, 2019–October 25, 2019*, Rpt to Cong., 15 Nov 2019, 2–4, https://www.dodig.mil/reports.html/Article/2020066/lead-inspector-general-for-operation-inherent-resolve-i-quarterly-report-to-the, Hist Files, CMH; Kareem Fahim, Karen DeYoung, and Susannah George, "Trump Says a Limited Number of Troops Will Remain in Syria After Ordering a Complete Withdrawal," *Washington Post*, 21 Oct 2019, https://www.washingtonpost.com/world/middle_east/us-discussing-proposal-to-leave-troops-around-syrias-oil-fields-pentagon-says/2019/10/21/0b024d4c-f401-11e9-8cf0-4cc99f74d127_story.html, Hist Files, CMH; Kyle Rempfer, "Why the Army Pulled Bradleys Out of Syrian Oil Fields After One Month," *Army Times*, 30 Jan 2020, https://www.armytimes.com/news/your-army/2020/01/30/why-the-army-pulled-bradleys-out-of-syrian-oil-fields-after-one-month/, Hist Files, CMH.

320. Jim Garamone, "Central Command Chief Gives Details on Baghdadi Raid," DoD News, 30 Oct 2019, https://www.defense.gov/Explore/News/Article/Article/2003960/central-command-chief-gives-details-on-baghdadi-raid/, Hist Files, CMH.

321. Shawn Snow, "New in 2020: Will Trump Pull the US Military out of Iraq and Syria?" *Military Times*, 29 Dec 2019, https://www.militarytimes.com/flashpoints/2019/12/29/new-in-2020-will-trump-pull-the-us-military-out-of-iraq-and-syria/, Hist Files, CMH.

322. W.J. Hennigan and Kimberly Dozier, "Iraqis Push for U.S. Troop Withdrawal in Symbolic Vote," *Time*, 5 Jan 2020, https://time.com/5759101/iraqi-parliament-vote-for-us-withdrawal/, Hist Files, CMH.

323. Joseph L. Votel and Eero R. Keravuori, "The By-With-Through Operational Approach," *Joint Force Quarterly* 89 (2nd Qtr 2018): 40.

324. J. Patrick Work, "Fighting the Islamic State By, With, and Through: How Mattered as Much as What," *Joint Force Quarterly* 89 (2nd Qtr 2018): 56–57.

325. Interv, Lt. Col. Scott C. Hammond, ARCENT, with Lt. Col. (Aus.) Stuart

Cree, Ch, Future Opns (CJ35), CJFLCC-OIR, n.d. [2016], 3, Hist Files, CMH.

326. Unclassified redaction of Park, *Narrative History of Combined Joint Task Force—Operation Inherent Resolve*, 3.

327. Witty, *Iraq's Post-2014 Counter Terrorism Service*, 7–11, 64.

328. Kogon, *Sky Dragon Dismantles the "Caliphate*,*"* 39.

329. "After Liberation Came Destruction: Iraqi Militias and the Aftermath of Amerli," Human Rights Watch, 18 Mar 2015, https://www.hrw.org/report/2015/03/18/after-liberation-came-destruction/iraqi-militias-and-aftermath-amerli, Hist Files, CMH; "Ruinous Aftermath: Militias Abuses Following Iraq's Recapture of Tikrit," Human Rights Watch, 20 Sep2015, https://www.hrw.org/report/2015/09/20/ruinous-aftermath/militias-abuses-following-iraqs-recapture-tikrit, Hist Files, CMH; "Iraq: Fallujah Abuses Inquiry Mired in Secrecy," Human Rights Watch, 7 Jul 2016, https://www.hrw.org/news/2016/07/07/iraq-fallujah-abuses-inquiry-mired-secrecy, Hist Files, CMH.

330. DoD Press Release, "Casualty Status as of 10 a.m. EDT March 29, 2019," 29 Mar 2019, https://dod.defense.gov/News/Casualty-Status/ (page discontinued), Hist Files, CMH.

JOINT TASK FORCE

Organizational Chart 2014–2015

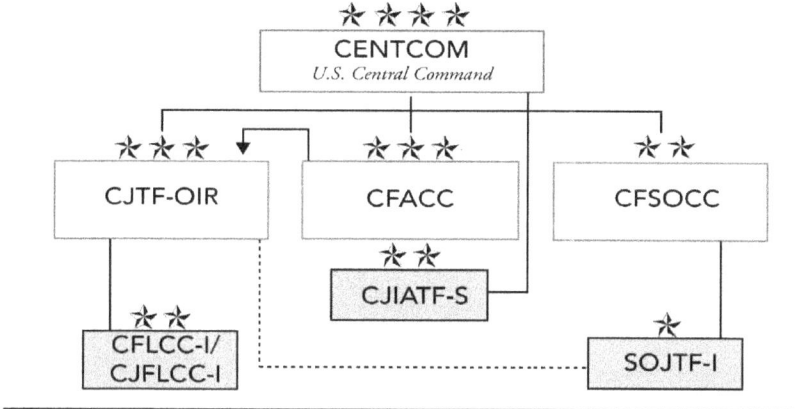

★ ★ ★ ★

CENTCOM
U.S. Central Command

★ ★ ★

CJTF-OIR

★ ★ ★

CFACC

★ ★

CFSOCC

★ ★

CFLCC-I/ CJFLCC-I

★ ★

CJIATF-S

★

SOJTF-I

JOINT TASK FORCE

Organizational Chart 2015–2017

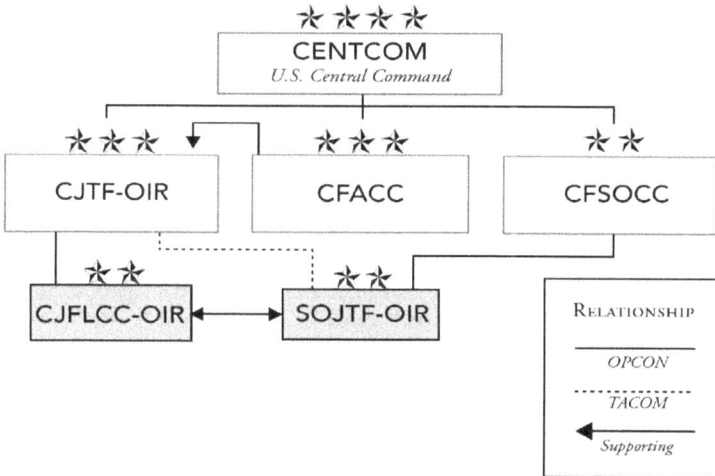

★ ★ ★ ★

CENTCOM
U.S. Central Command

★ ★ ★

CJTF-OIR

★ ★ ★

CFACC

★ ★

CFSOCC

★ ★

CJFLCC-OIR ◄──► **SOJTF-OIR**

RELATIONSHIP
———— *OPCON*
----------- *TACOM*
◄—— *Supporting*

JOINT TASK FORCE

Organizational Chart 2018–Present

APPENDIX 3

⭐⭐⭐⭐
CENTCOM
U.S. Central Command

⭐⭐⭐
CJTF-OIR

⭐⭐⭐
CFACC

⭐⭐
CFSOCC

⭐⭐
SOJTF-OIR

RELATIONSHIP

OPCON

TACOM

Supporting

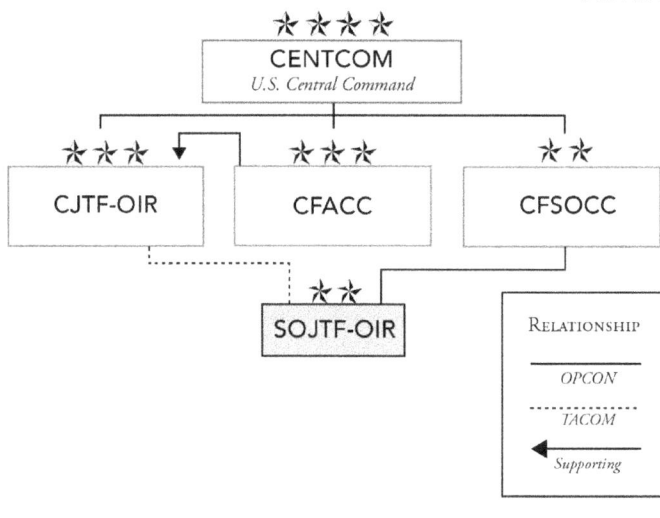

ABBREVIATIONS

CFACC	Combined Forces Air Component Commander
CFLCC-I	Combined Forces Land Component Command–Iraq
CFSOCC	Combined Forces Special Operations Component Command
CJFLCC-I	Combined Joint Forces Land Component Command–Iraq
CJFLCC-OIR	Combined Joint Forces Land Component Command–Operation INHERENT RESOLVE
CJIATF-S	Combined Joint Interagency Task Force–Syria
CJTF-OIR	Combined Joint Task Force–Operation INHERENT RESOLVE
SOJTF-I	Special Operations Joint Task Force–Iraq
SOJTF-OIR	Special Operations Joint Task Force–Operation INHERENT RESOLVE

114

OPERATION EAGLE STRIKE
Task Organization, October 2016

XXX
CJTF-OIR

XXXX
CJOC

XX
CJFLCC-OIR

XXX
CJOC Forward

Peshmerga
XX KSF
X KSF
X KSF
X KSF

X
101

XX
PMF

Eastern Axis
XX CTS
X CTS
X CTS
•••
|| ERU
|| ERU

Southeastern Axis
XX
9th
X 35 | 9
X 3
X 36 | 9
|| ERU
|| ERU

Northern Axis
XX 16th
X 73 | 16
X 75 | 16
•••
|| ERU
|| ERU

Southwestern Axis
XX FEDPOL 5th
XX 15th
XX ERU
X 3 | 5
X 34 | 9
X 1 ERU
X 4 | 5
X 75 | 15
X 2 ERU
X 4 | 5
X 36 | 9
X ERU
X 5 | 5
|| ERU
X 6 | 5
|| ERU
X 5

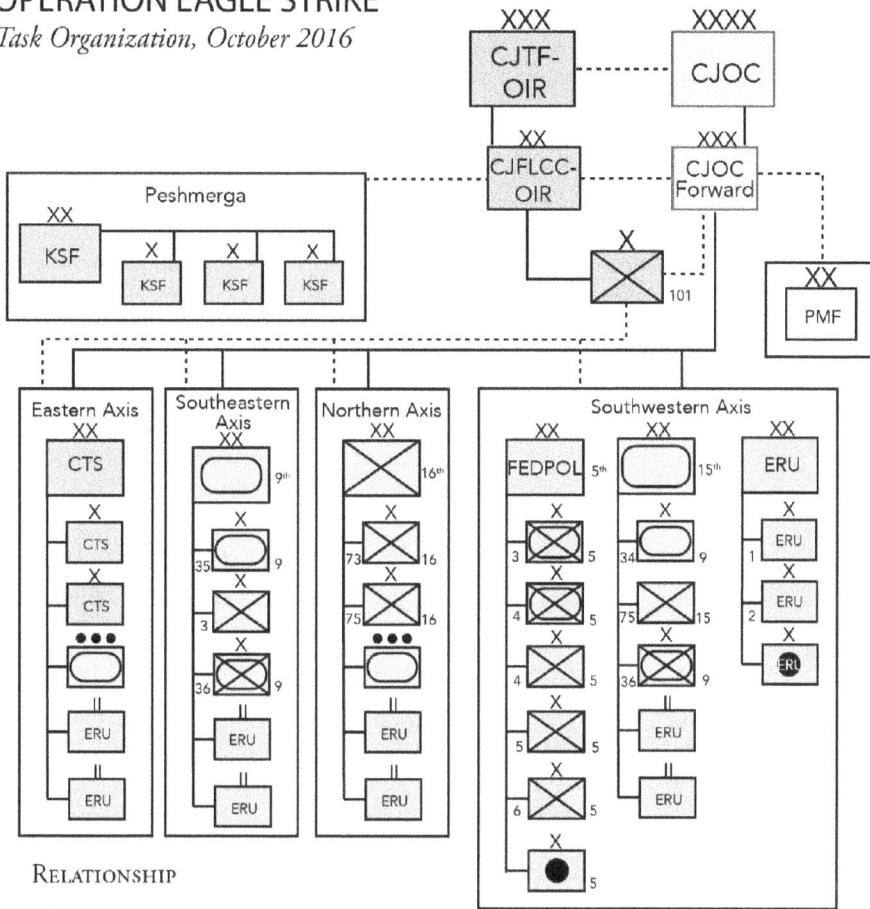

RELATIONSHIP

Operational Control

Coordination

Iraqi Army

Iraqi Federal Police

Iraqi Counter Terrorism Service

Coalition Units

Peshmerga

ISF Joint Commands

X   Brigade || Battalion/ Squadron
XX   Division   •••   Platoon/ Detachment
XXX   Corps

Infantry Mechanized/Armored

Field Artillery

Armor Unit

Infantry Unit

THE AUTHOR

Mason W. Watson is a historian at the U.S. Army Center of Military History (CMH), where he specializes in contemporary U.S. military operations and the history of the Iraq War. He joined CMH in 2017 as a graduate research assistant and worked for more than a year as a member of CMH's World War I Commemoration Committee, coauthoring a commemorative brochure on the Second Battle of the Marne, *The Marne, 15 July–6 August 1918* (2018). He holds a BA in history from the College of William and Mary and an MA and a PhD in military history from the Ohio State University.

FURTHER READINGS

Harris, William. *Quicksilver War: Syria, Iraq and the Spiral of Conflict.* London: Hurst, 2018.

Hashim, Ahmed. *The Caliphate at War: Operational Realities and Innovations of the Islamic State.* New York: Oxford University Press, 2018.

Lambeth, Benjamin S. *Airpower in the War against ISIS.* Annapolis, MD: Naval Institute Press, 2021.

Lister, Charles R. *The Syrian Jihad: Al-Qaeda, the Islamic State and the Evolution of an Insurgency.* London: Hurst, 2017.

Mumford, Andrew. *The West's War against Islamic State: Operation Inherent Resolve in Syria and Iraq.* London: I. B. Tauris, 2021.

Pittard, Dana J. H., and Wes J. Bryant. *Hunting the Caliphate: America's War on ISIS and the Dawn of the Strike Cell.* New York: Post Hill Press, 2019.

Rayburn, Joel D., and Frank K. Sobchak, eds. *The U.S. Army in the Iraq War.* 2 vols. Carlisle, PA: Strategic Studies Institute and U.S. Army War College Press, 2019.

Verini, James. *They Will Have to Die Now: Mosul and the Fall of the Caliphate.* New York: W. W. Norton, 2019.

This monograph is a preliminary history of this campaign; a more detailed account is in preparation. To assist the author in fully capturing the U.S. Army's role in the operation, CMH encourages readers to send comments, corrections, and additional information via email to usarmy.mcnair.cmh.mbx.answers@army.mil or via mail to 102 Fourth Ave., Fort McNair, DC 20319.

www.ingramcontent.com/pod-product-compliance
Lightning Source LLC
Chambersburg PA
CBHW080059280326

41935CB00030B/1694